# Micro and Macro Deteri … n



**Ashok A. Shrotriy**

## CONTENT

# CHAPTER – I
# INTRODUCTION

All economic activities are centered on man; hence, population is the principal factor affecting the economic development of any country. Adam Smith considered man as "*a form of capital*". Prof. Marshal also thought of man as center of all economic activities. He said that the purpose of economics is to be related to the study of man in ordinary business of life. Thus, "*all human behaviours are influenced by economics*" (Ghosh 1993). T.W. Schultz, Gary Becker, H.L Leibenstein, Colin Clark, Harbinson, A.G.B. Fisher – all these economists have explained that human behaviours are amenable to economics. Ghosh (1993) notes, "*The growth of population affects, directly or indirectly, every aspect of social and economic life. Population growth itself is conditioned by economic factors.*" Further, he points out, "*The rate of growth of population affects the national income, per capita income, investment, saving and standard of living.*"

Both quantitative and qualitative changes in population growth and human resources are the decisive factors of economic development. Changes in GNP, per capita GNP, welfare and social indicators of development are also directly and indirectly connected with quality and size of population. Hence population growth is both cause and result of economic development. The role-played by these factors in the economic development of developed and developing countries varies considerably. Especially rapid population growth in developing countries like India has impeded economic development. If the rate of population growth is greater than the rate of economic development, it brings down per capita income of a nation. If the rate of economic development is more than the rate of population growth, it results in the increase in per capita income. So, if the rate of population growth is controlled, economic development can be achieved more rapidly

Growth in population increases effective demands but it may not be possible to meet all demands. On the other hand, it also exerts pressure on existing infrastructure. The infrastructure includes education, health, housing, clothing, roads, means of communication, quick and effective transportation etc. This requires more capital investments. But in developing countries, a large part of the total available investible resources have to be utilised to meet basic needs of people and as a consequence, less capital is available for investment in creating infrastructure. On these circumstances, population control is a desirable option for economic development. Gerald Meier (1984) points out, "*In these countries (poor countries), per capita income has remained pitifully low, and the alarming prospects population growth have revived neo Malthusian fears. Once again there is a widespread concern that economic betterment will be thwarted by excessive population pressure and that, unless acceptable means are found for checking population growth, 'the revolution of rising expectations' must remain unfulfilled. It has become widely acceptable that the development problem is one of increasing the fertility of the soil and reducing the fertility of human beings*". Meier puts emphasis on finding effective measures for checking population growth because if population growth is not controlled it will be very difficult to accelerate the pace of economic development.

It has been observed that there is a vast difference in the size, composition and distribution of population in developing countries. There is population explosion because of vast differences between birth rate and death rate, i.e. birth rate is quite high while death rate is low. Keenleyside comments that the effects of population on world economy are deadlier than a bomb explosion. He comments, rather in a lighter vein, "*The womb is slower than the bomb but it may prove just as deadly. Suffocation rather than incineration may mark the end of the human story.*" We may not be as pessimists as Keenleyside over our concern regarding population explosion but his note of caution to the whole of humanity cannot be overlooked viewing the rapid growth of population in the South Asian countries like India, Pakistan, Bangladesh, etc. The rate of population growth in developing countries is about 2% whereas in developed countries it is about 1%. In developed countries, the rate of population below the age group of 15 years is 40% whereas in developing countries it is 20% to 25%. In developing countries, 90% of the dependent population is children while in rich countries it is 66%. From the composition of age-wise distribution of population in the developing countries, it can be argued that in future also the population growth might prove to be an obstacle in economic development because of several reasons as mentioned earlier.

Education and training are the two very important factors among others, which can enhance stock of human capital. It also needs more investments. Training and education improve work efficiency and mobility of the labour force. The changes like these are of vital importance in economic development. V.G. Mankar (1995) observes, "*An improvement in the quality of human resources is important as investment in physical capital.*" Human beings are motivated for economic development through new ideas, objectives and aspirations. Meier considers development of human resources as one of the strategies of economic development. "*If the earlier faith in development through accumulation of material capital has waned, it is now widely believed that improvement in the quality of people as productive agents must be the central objective of development policies*" (Meier, 1984).

Most of the development economists lay emphasis on the betterment of human beings as instrumental to economic development. Their concern over the problem of population can be largely classified as under: (1) high rate of population growth, (2) high dependency ratio, (3) high birth rate, (4) high infant mortality and (5) lack of proper training and education. These will provide guideline for the further discussion of the problem.

## 1.1 Population Growth

The world population has crossed six billion mark. The total world population between 1981 and 1990 was 4307 million, which grew to 5736 million between 1991 and 1997. The annual rate of population growth between 1981 and 1990 was 1.8 per cent, which reduced to 1.4 per cent during 1991-97.

The general trends of population indicate that population growth in developing countries is more rapid than in developed countries. During 1981-90 and 1991-97, the population growth rate in the developed countries was 0.6 per cent, which shows a steady growth rate, while in the developing countries it was 1.7 per cent. This was obviously higher than that of the developed countries (UN/DESA, 1998).

India is one of the developing countries of the world. India possesses about 2.4 per cent of the world's land area and 14.6 per cent of the total of the world's population. The total population of India in 1991 was 84.63 million. In 2001, India crossed one billion populations. In the year 2016 it is expected to be 126.4 crore. The annual population growth rate of India was 2.14 per cent in 1991. The annual population growth rate went down from 2.28 per cent in 1981 to 2.14 percent in 1991. Yet, India is the second highest populous country in the world.

Gujarat is one of the highly populous states of India. Gujarat has a total area of 196024 square kilometers. Gujarat has registered a 22.66 per cent growth rate as compared to 21.19 per cent recorded in 1991. According to 2001, census record the population of Gujarat has reached to 5,05,96,992 as against 4,13,09,582 recorded in 1991. Gujarat is also one of the advanced states of India. Urbanization is very high in Gujarat. The state has the second highest urban population. It possesses 34.49 per cent of urban population while the rate of urban population in the whole of India was 25.72 per cent in the year 1991. Considering each urban agglomeration as one unit, the total numbers of urban units recorded in 1991 were 264. Surat city possesses the second highest number of population in the state. The fast developing city of Gujarat, it has registered 62.38 percent growth rate taking the figure of the industrial hub to 24,33,785 from 15 lakh in 1991. Surat has total area of 111.16 square kilometers (SMC). It is an expanding city. During the last 27 years the area of the city has ,almost doubled. The detailed demographic characteristics and relevant socio-economic characteristics of India, Gujarat and Surat are described in chapter three.

## 1.2 Demographic Transition

The changes that take place between the differences in birth rate and death rate are known as demographic transition. Frank W. Notestein presented the theory of demographic transition in 1945. He expressed the theory through changes in fertility. This transitions starts in the initial phase of economic development of a country. The European countries at present are in their last phase of demographic transition because in these countries, both birth and death rates are low and the differences between these two rates are almost negligible. A.J. Coale and Edger M. Hoover (1959) said, "*the change in the birth and death rates are obviously associated with economic development.*" But India is still far behind these countries. India entered the second phase of demographic transition after 1921. From the early 20$^{th}$ century to the end of the century the difference between birth rate and death rate remained high for considerable period in India, and to day, in 2001, India is on the verge of completion of this second stage of demographic transition. It has been observed that in the last few years, both birth rate and death rate are declining and the gap between the two is also gradually narrowing. Hence, the efforts to regulate population growth in the recent past are concentrated on bringing about a noticeable decline in birth rate. It is said that the socio-economic and cultural factors are responsible for the high birth rate. Hence, the study of the level of birth rate and its determinants is one of the crucial topics of research and is relevant even today.

Socio-economic characteristics affect the size and combination of population. The size and combination of population decide the rate and quality of population. All these help in the study of demographic characteristics. These are discussed in demographic transition theory.

Fertility, mortality and migration – these three are the decisive factors of population growth. The changes taking place in population growth due to fertility and mortality are natural, while changes in population growth due to migration are artificial. The various factors affecting fertility, mortality and migration provide a varied scope to study population patterns and growth. These are known as demographic variables.

The study of demographic variables is important both at rural level and urban level, because changes in these variables help to explain population growth with reference to changes in the patterns of biological, social and economic factors. Demographic variables are more active in urban areas than in rural areas because in urban areas economic development is very rapid.

### 1.3 Surat Population Study

Population studies are required to be undertaken on regular basis. They are basically quantitative and qualitative is nature. These studies help to understand the dynamics of population growth and formulate appropriate policy measures to contain population growth. Demographers have propounded population theories from their population studies conducted during different time periods.

Several studies are undertaken to examine factors affecting population growth. These factors are likely to differ in different regions. Over a period of time the importance of some of these factors have also changed. The aim of the present study is to examine the importance of socio-economic factors, which can have bearings on population growth. Primary data (micro level) are used for this purpose. Macro level data are also used to understand the dynamics underlying population growth.

The present study entitled population growth: Micro and Macro Determinants, is based on Surat. Surat has been selected for this study for various reasons. Some of them are as cited here. The city has experienced a record growth rate of population during the last decade. It will be interesting to examine the pattern of growth and factors responsible for higher population growth in Surat.

Till to day many theories have been put forward to explain factors affecting population growth. The former theories have been modified by cultural patterns while the later or modern theories are strongly influenced by economic and social factors. Both former and later theories explain the role of supply of children and demand for children. The supply, demand and regulation are the three basic components of fertility, which are decisive components of population growth.

### 1.4 Supply of Children

Supply of children means natural fertility which is defined by the number of surviving children a couple would have without any deliberate attempt to regulate fertility Bongarts (1963), Bula and Lee (1983), Easterline (1978). Natural fertility is a function of both behavioural and biological factors of child survival (Potter 1963).

In India, marriage is one of the most important social institutions. Married men and women have a different status in society. Births occurred within marriage become socially acceptable. Marriages occurring at a younger age create a longer period for supply of children. It enhances natural marital fertility. According to Bongarts and Menken (1983), natural marital fertility is determined by several variables, which affect the length of NMF (Natural Marital Fertility). These variables are: (i) the period of postpartum infecundability, (ii) the period of natural fertility (waiting time for conception), (iii) intra-uterine mortality risk and (iv) permanent sterility.

Earlier population theories highlight the relationship between age at marriage and natural marital fertility. Malthus also mentioned that early age marriage is responsible for excessive population growth. Malthus believed that late marriage is an essential preventive check on fertility and population growth. Early marriages lengthen the total period of married life. This provides a long span for reproductive activity. Couples become parents at an early age, hence the gap between the two generations becomes narrow. This factor is responsible for population growth.

## 1.5 Demand for Children

The demand for children refers to the voluntary control of births. Parents can plan to have desired number of children. Voluntary control and planned parenthood make up demand. The demand for children depends upon the willingness of parents. Couples have their own understanding of the value of children. Their understanding obviously influences the demand for children, which in turn is influenced by the structural features of society.

The demand for children depends upon the number of children, i.e. family size. First birth gender, interval between two surviving children, the education they should receive and such similar matters also play an important role in determining the family size (Lee 1993). Many theories are propounded to explain factors affecting demand for children. The Household Utility Maximising Model (Leibenstein 1907, Easterline 1975, Becker 1976) is a well-known and quite useful model in understanding parents' decision in determining the number of children in the family. Liebenstein published "*Economic Backwardness and Economic Growth*" in 1557. He formulated a theory that can explain the factors, which determine the number of children desired by each couple. The Household Utility Maximising Approach suggests that parents' utilities for having children is derived from their idea of security in the old age. It can be assumed that utility from these sources increase at decreasing rate.

### 1.6 Lebenstein, Easterline and Backer's Theories

The population theories of Leibenstein, Easterline and Becker are helpful in understanding the dynamics of population growth in developing countries. In the underdeveloped countries parents view children as a source of productive utility. In other words they consider children as a source of income. But they oversee the fact that they might enhance economic burden. They do not think that an additional child in the family enhances direct and indirect cost. Generally, in a traditional society where economic burden mostly falls on agriculture, this type of attitude is common; but in a structured society of urban areas, the concept of fertility is totally different. In urban societies income effects, survival effects and occupational effects play a vital role, hence both direct and indirect cost of child rearing is greater than that of the rural-traditional communities. According to Becker's Economic Analysis of Fertility (1960), fertility increases with the increase in income but this does not affect the quality of children. To enhance the quality of children parents are required to spend more on child rearing along with their increased income. Hence, the number of children should be less, to provide them better standard of living. This means the demand for children is actually less with the increase in parents' income. According to Easterline (1969), fertility behaviour is influenced by the interplay between aspirations of parents and the resources they have to satisfy their aspirations.

### 1.7 Parents' Preference for Male Child

In many cases, couples prefer more sons than daughters (Mukherjee, 1973), Sharma and Jain (1974). Some couples often prefer to have at least one son in their family, while some others prefer to have balance in their gender choice; i.e. one son and one daughter. Probability of desire to have sons in the family also influences fertility. Viewing the fertility criteria from economic point of view, it has been observed that the labour force of the urban area do not think either about their own standard of living or the standard of living of their children. They spend less on child rearing. Even to day they consider children as economic assets, hence they are indifferent between a male and female child. It is the service class people who are always worried about both the gender and the number of children in their families. They normally prefer one son/one daughter balance. The standard of living of the educated class is high. It has been observed that they are not concerned about the gender of their child, but they generally prefer one or two children in the family, irrespective of their gender.

The cultural influence on demand for children is quite similar both in rural and urban area. Generally people have strong preference for a son as their legal heir. As per cultural ethics, there is generally a wide gap between the ages of husband and wife. Wives are normally younger than their husbands, hence the chances of their being widows are also more. They expect a boy in the family as an old age security after husband's death. Leibenstein had also considered the demand for children as a source of old age security in the theory of population. Emancipated women in urban areas desire less number of children so that they can spare time for their desired activities or jobs, hence they prefer less children in the family, irrespective of their gender (Chaudhari 1982, Clepend 1983 and Das 1987).

### 1.8 The Effect of Regulation Over Replacement

Both regulation and replacement of children in a family affect fertility. The regulation effect limits the demand for children, but at the same time in the case of the death of a child, parents want another child; i.e. replacement. In that case the period of fertility becomes longer. Generally in urban areas, the newly wed couples decide on a particular time limit to expand their family. This is known as birth interval. They plan their family in such a way that they can give maximum time to child rearing, hence they prefer a comparatively short gap between the births of two children. After this planned birth interval they avoid both conception and childbirth. This directly controls their fertility. Of course, replacement and preference of sons over daughters do affect fertility (Rustein and Medica, 1978, Preston 1975-78, Chaudhari 1962). Because of the uncertainty of child survival, sometimes parents prefer more children than they actually desire to have, so that a desired number of children remain in the family in a long run. This uncertainly of survival also increases demand for more children.

In urban areas fertility norms of the people vary a great deal according to their economic and social status. These variations affect mortality rate. In the high income group mortality rate is found very low. Their reproductive norms are quite different from other lower income group of people. Even to day mortality rate is very high in the low-income group. Infant mortality and child mortality is even higher in this group; hence, they produce more number of children (Chaudhari, 1982).

## 1.9 Population Growth and Socio-Economic Determinants

Population growth is mainly explained by socio-economic factors, as they are the major factors affecting population growth. Generally, these factors do not affect the birth of the first child in a family, but they affect every next childbirth. This is true for both individual couples as well as for the society as a whole. These factors are more important in the study of fertility trends in the urban area. These reflect social changes, aptitude of people, individual's behaviour as well as the effects of modernization on individuals and society. Time and again, the various studies on population growth have tried to show that socio-economic factors have greatly affected and are still affecting population growth.

The major socio-economic factors affecting population growth are: religion, education, age (particularly mother's) at marriage, religion, occupation, level of income, type of family, migrant or non-migrant status of people, and their residential facilities.

## 1.10 Religion

Religion plays an important role in shaping the attitude of a person. The grip of religion on individuals and their beliefs has been very strong. It has been a very strong factor affecting fertility, directly and indirectly; hence it has been known as one of the important factors affecting individuals and their beliefs regarding children and childbirths. Almost all religions accept childbirth as a gift of nature or of God, but a son is given more importance in all religious acts. According to Hindu religion, marriage should take place before an individual enters the period of fertility (especially in case of females) – (Singh 1986, Mahadevan 1986, Arora 1983-86). Religions and caste factors play equal role both in rural as well as in urban areas, but in urban areas the intensity of these factors is comparatively low because of socio-economic developments and the changes in social environment. Several studies indicating fertility behaviour of various religious and caste groups have been undertaken in India. The findings of these studies are interesting to note. These studies indicate that Muslims have higher fertility than Christians. The socio-economically stronger class people have low fertility compared to the fertility rate of socio-economically weak people. (UN 1961, Driver 1963, Wyon and Gordon 1965, Bhanot and Gandotra 1971, Bele and Kanitkar 1977).

Constitutional changes in the families are taking place along with socio-economic developments. The gap between the social status of men and women is becoming narrow and fertility rate is decreasing. The important of religion seems to be gradually declining.

### 1.11 The Size of Family

The size of family directly affects fertility. Joint family; nuclear family and extended family types show variations in fertility rate. It has been observed that in joint families generally early age marriages take place because the newly wed couples are not directly burdened by various family responsibilities. As a result of early marriage, they also acquire early parental status without direct economic and social responsibilities. Caste and income also play important role in deciding age at marriage. In joint family system, one can expect the rate of fertility to be higher. In other words, joint family system boosts fertility (Loriner 1954, Burch and Gendall 1970, Caldwell 1981, Chaudhari 1982). It has also been observed that in the extended family type fertility rate decreases because such families have particular beliefs regarding sex. Moreover, their customs and traditions, the environment of their locale etc. are also responsible factors (Nag 1981, Karkal 1972, Ramu 1988). Even after all these studies and observations, it cannot be asserted that there is direct relationship between fertility and family type.

### 1.12 Education

Education is another variable that influences fertility decision. The level of education amongst men and women is almost equal in cities, therefore fertility in urban people is lower than in rural population. The highly educated population in cities possesses still lower fertility than average urban dwellers (Minkler 1970, Hermalin and Mason 1980, Berent 1983).

Educated people tend to think about their future and plan their families accordingly. They are also worried about their social and economic status. They try to upgrade their standard of living after acquiring the desired status. They are worried about the maintenance of that high standard. Moreover, they also wish that their children must also maintain at least the status that they inherit from their parents. Hence, it can reasonably be stated that education does affect fertility indirectly, as educated people do not wish to bring any more undesired children in their family. For this purpose, educated people first regularise fertility with altering the supply and demand for children. They prefer small family. Education also stimulates other determinant, like social, economic and demographic. In other words, education acts like oxygen. It is a catalytic factor (Caldwell 1978-80, Easterline 1976, 1963, Stycos 1978).

Education is considered to be very important factor for economic development. Its effects can be seen both at micro and macro levels. Its effects on the individuals can be studied through primary data collected at household level. According to Leibensteinian theory of population, expenditure on child rearing increases with increase in income. Marginal utility acquired from the marginal child decreases. Child consumption utility decreases with the increased survival rate and opportunity relative cost increases. According to cost and benefit analysis, parents' economic utility also decreases. On the other hand, parents have to spend more after children's education (Becker 1960, Easterline 1969, Dyson and Moore 1963, Mason 1984).

Educated parents always try to provide better housing comforts to their children. Good housing condition include ventilated, lightened minimum required place to comfortably accommodate each member of the family. Educated people also can have better understanding of hygiene and sanitation problems. Education also helps people in maintaining balance of economic condition with better nutritional and health conditions, hence it is believed that in the urban area environmental and hygienic conditions are good compared to rural area. But this is only true where people are economically sound and educated. In city slums, people live even in a worse condition compared to the rural dwellers. IMR and MMR are gradually reducing. There are lesser opportunities of child replacement with addition of another child in a family. Education also provides adequate knowledge and awareness of contraception and thus influences supply of children. The supply of children is also influenced and checked by other factors like extended age at marriage, duration of breast-feeding, contraception, sterilization, etc. The awareness of all these come through education. Educated people prefer temporary methods of contraception, so that they succeed in maintaining the desired gap between the birth of two children. Abortion also helps to check the supply of children, but it is not desirable as it is not very healthy. It affects adversely on the health of both individuals and society. Partly educated parents and other family members insist upon male child in the family but even they cannot overlook the family size. Thus, education moulds the minds of people a great deal. The demand for children is found to be reducing in urban areas because of the changing attitudes of people regarding family size, and the cost benefit analysis applied in rearing children. Reduction in IMR and MMR would make demand for children low (Cadwell and M.C. Donald 1982, Hobcraft 1983).

India is passing through the second stage of socio-economic development. In this phase of development there are many variations in socio-economic sectors. The urbanisation process in India is also passing through its second stage alongwith its socio-economic development; hence, there are large-scale variations or inequalities in social and economic formation. Several studies have been conducted and are being conducted to find out how inverse relationship between education and fertility affects the population growth in India (UN 1961, Driver 1963, Sharma and Misra 1978, Jain 1981). A large section of people in the cities are still uneducated and illiterate. Thus there is an imbalance between the educational status of the people in cities. Though there are several opportunities and options available in the urban area, people are unable to avail of these opportunities as at least

30% of the urban population lives in slums. Studies of the slums indicate that in the class who are devoid of proper education, the rate of fertility is high. But with the expansion of formal education fertility rate is gradually decreasing. Thus education affects the size of family. The study of the rate of highest education, the rate of average educated individuals and the rate of educated women in a family also play a major role in deciding the family size.

### 1.13 Occupational and Income Status

A lot of vividness and variety in the occupational status of people is found in the urban area. The occupational status plays a major role in population growth. Occupational status of the people and natural population growth are found to be interrelated. The occupation type of people has both direct and indirect effects on fertility. Some families in the cities enjoy industrial status. In such families, the male work force is generally of permanent type. In mixed industrial status families there are also service-class individuals. Generally, women are engaged in services in the mixed industrial status families. It has been observed that in the families with self-employment status both males and females have equal shares. Such variations in family status also affect fertility. Occupational status of a family also plays its part in deciding the age at marriage. Even the chances of child mortality depend upon family's occupation status because of the following reasons: (1) Cost and benefits of children depend upon parents' income (2) Parents' income depends upon their occupation type or employment. In the families engaged in small and cottage industries, families of ordinary labour force, families with disguised or under-employed individuals, fertility rate is found to be high. Thus it can be said that occupational status and the rate of fertility are closely linked.

Like other factors occupation also affects supply of and demand for children. In urban areas, people try to improve their occupation status by shifting from traditional to modern occupations. Both men and women are engaged in their occupations. This naturally increases the age at marriage of the spouses. Economic progress of the parents reduces the requirement and expectation of economic benefits to be derived from children. With the rise in income and the standard of living, quality of children and not the quantity of children is desired. This helps to bring down IMR and Child Mortality. Parents can provide good nutritive food and can take better care of their children's health. According to population growth models provided by Becker and Easterline, aspirations of parents about their children's future help to check the number of children in their family. It has been observed that in India also shifts in occupational status have lowered fertility. (UN 1961, Driver 1961, Srinivasan 1967, Arora 1963, Muthiah 1984).

### 1.14 Migration

Population growth in the urban agglomerations is affected by both reproductive changes and net immigration. In the process of urbanisation the increase in urban population is not only a result of reproductive changes in the people but also due to population migration, e.g. in 2001 the growth rate of population in Surat was 6.6 per cent but the natural growth rate of population was comparatively low. Economic development takes place in the initial phase of urbanisation process. Progress in trade and commerce and provision of various economic activities provide the cause for population migration. Both pull and push factors are responsible for population migration. Pull factor is responsible for the migration of people from the thickly populous places to comparatively less populated areas because in such places there are more and better employment opportunities available. Europeans migrated to America, Australia and Africa where the supply of land was ample and the pressure of population on the land was not at all excessive. There are better job opportunities and more economic possibilities in such places. There are also better facilities of housing, education and health. These things help people to upgrade their standard of living. Moreover, less populated places provide good atmosphere to the dwellers.

Pull factors attract people towards new places, while push factors force people to migrate. Factors like poverty, inadequate job opportunities, unemployment and underemployment, low standard of living, etc. in the native land push people to migrate from their homeland. Even religious and political factors are also responsible for migration. Moreover, chances of personal development, better job opportunities, marriage, etc. are also responsible factors for individual or group migrations.

The total population of Surat city in the year 2001 (estimated figure according to census 2001) is 24 lakh. Out of these, four lakh people are migrated from Saurashtra. This is a case of intra-state migration. Almost eight lakh people in Surat are from the Northern states of India while four lakh people are from the Southern India. These migratory people make Surat a multi-cultural place. In case of Surat, migration has become a mass movement because infiltration of population is a continuous process.

### 1.15 Health Status and Family Planning

The health status of a population is determined by various factors like per capita income, nutrition, water supply, sanitation, housing amenities, health services available to the community, response of people in availing these facilities, morbidity rate, climate, percentage of population below poverty line (PBPL), structure of the economy etc. From the study of these factors, the health status of a population can be decided.

Family planning is another subject of vital importance in understanding the issues related to population growth. Both individuals and people in general are directly concerned with family planning. For individuals family planning is voluntary, but when mass is involved it becomes a part of population policy of the state, because the governments as well NGOs are directly involved. Here again education plays an important role. Educated individuals are generally aware of the importance of family planning but same thing cannot be said about illiterate people. For such population family planning is implemented as a part of population policy. Even in cities 100% of population, do not accept family planning. One of the main reasons is that most of the migrant people are illiterate or barely literate, and because they do not have inadequate income.

Family planning methods include permanent sterilization and temporary contraceptive devices. These devices are rubber contraceptives, oral pills, loop, diaphragm, jelly etc. Some contraceptives are not very effective and some others are highly expensive; while some are simple, harmless and effective but not very convenient. Sterilization is a permanent solution from the occurrence of pregnancy. Male sterilization is simpler and safer than female sterilisation. But in India males are not ready to come forward willingly for such operations because of certain beliefs and because the Indian society is a male dominated society. Abstinence from conjugal relationship is neither advisable nor practically possible. Hence, it is necessary to find some way to check population growth.

### 1.16 Objectives of the Study

The broad objectives of the present study are as follows:

(1) To study fertility variations among different groups (a) permanent dwellers and (b) recently migrated population.

(2) To examine the role of religion on population growth.

(3) To examine the impact of income/standard of living on family size.

(4) To study how education affects population growth.

(5) To study how occupational structure affects population growth.

(6) To examine the role of family planning on population growth.

(7) To look for policy measure based on present study.

### 1.17 Hypotheses of the Study

In the light of the above-cited objectives of the study and on the basis of review of literature, some testable hypotheses were formulated. These hypotheses in a broad perspective are: (1) Fertility rate in the recently migrated population is higher than those who are permanent dwellers. (2) There are significant variations in family size among religious groups. (3) Nuclear families have fewer number of children. (4) Cost of rearing children is inversely related to family size. (5) Level of income/standard of living is inversely related to family size. (6) Level of literacy is inversely related to family size. (7) Persons employed in unorganised sector will have larger families.

## 1.18 Organization of the Thesis

This thesis consists of six chapters. The details of each chapter is given below:

*Chapter-II: Theory of population Growth*

Population theories are enumerated in this chapter. The enumerated population theories are Pre-Malthusian theories, Malthusian theory, Biological theories, Social-cultural theories and Economic theories. Some of the testable hypotheses are derived from these population theories.

*Chapter-III: Demographic Profile*

The third chapter discusses socio economic characteristics and demographic profile of India and Gujarat in general and of Surat in particular.

*Chapter-IV: Research Methodology*

This chapter presents methodology of data collection. The description of sample household is also given. The chapter also includes discussion on statistical techniques used for this study.

*Chapter-V: Empirical Analysis of Micro Determinants of Population Growth*

This chapter deals with empirical analysis carried out to test the hypotheses. It has been tried to examine variation in number of children of families according to income groups and level of literacy groups.

Occupation type shows minor variations in number of children. Type of family seems to be one of the important factors in deciding the number of children in family size. However, income factors are taken as considerations. Significant variations across with religious groups have been found from this study.

*Chapter-VI: Summary and Policy Implications*

The sixth chapter deals with policy and conclusions derived from the study.

# CHAPTER – II

# POPULATION THEORIES AND POPULATION GROWTH

Population analysis helps in understanding the dynamics of growth and quality of population. Population theorists have at different times, provided explanations to understand the temporal and structural changes in population. They have expounded population theories with reference to the changing patterns in biological, military, political, social and economical factors. These theories help to decide whether the rate of total population is optimum or under or over.

Socio-economic development is one of the major factors affecting population growth. It has been observed that, in the initial stage of economic development population increases, but in the later stage of economic development, population growth decreases. Quality of population becomes more important later on. Thus, quality and not quantity of population increases. The above-cited changes in the pattern of population were first theorized by Laundry (1909) and Thompson (1929). They have stated that in the initial stage of development the rates of both fertility and mortality are high while in the later stage of development both these are low. These changes are based on cost benefit analyses. Parents prefer less children and more consumption.

However, this benefit analysis theory has now become less relevant, as the concept of socio-economic development has undergone a total change.

Population theories explain the changing patterns of population at different times. Economic development is associated with employment opportunities and education. At the same time life-style is changed, people tend to consume more, obligations towards family are altered; and with the changing social pattern responsibilities of parents towards family are also increased. Size and quality of family get priority; hence, nuclear family system is preferred to joint family system. Parents develop target-oriented approach as standard of life becomes higher; and as a result of this, extended family is no more preferred. As income increases the family enters into higher socio-economic group. To maintain this high standard less children are preferred by parents. These changing socio-economic factors – theoretically defined and explained by various demographers at different times – affect fertility and mortality.

## 2.1 Population Theories

Malthus is considered the initiator of population theory. Nevertheless, even before him economists and sociologists had expressed their views on population. The views expressed by them lacked methodological approach as they explained only the population conditions of the periods concerned, while Malthus' theory on population gained importance because it was more systematic in its approach. His theory became a landmark in population studies. The time before Malthus is known as Pre-Malthusian era.

## 2.2 Pre-Malthusian Thoughts

In ancient time, the study of population was only focused on quantitative aspect of population in which state politics played an important role, because increase in population provided the state an excuse to increase its geographical boundaries. This is the reason why increase in population was not considered to be a problem according to ancient thinkers of Greece like Plato (340 B.C.) and Aristotle (354 B.C.) (Charles, 1904). In Plato's view, the optimum urban population should be 50,000 inclusive of civilians, children and slaves. Xenophone opined that increase in population of a state brings benefit of labour division, bringing prosperity to the state. During the middle era of Roman Empire the problem of over population was raised by the thinkers of that period. In the $17^{th}$ and $18^{th}$ centuries Germany and Spain faced the problem of under population for decades. This was the initial period of mercantilism in the Western countries. In view of this problem of under population economists of the time greatly emphasized and advocated increase in population as a vital tool of economic progress. According to Eli Heckscher (1935), "*an almost frantic desire to increase population prevailed in all countries*" to make mercantilism a success. In the $17^{th}$ and $18^{th}$ centuries constant wars and increase in production were the two major reasons for the above stated opinion of Eli Heckscher. To cope with the problem of under population some steps were suggested. They are, (1) importance to the institution of marriage, (2) encouragement to large family, (3) social welfare, (4) steps to check migration of population. Economists of that time opined that in the situation of under population easy availability of resources make the population lazy. If population increases, people work harder and try to increase their resources to cope with their increasing needs. In the countries not gifted with gold and silver mines, export activity was encouraged to balance the mercantile equilibrium. This also required increase in population because quantity of labour was more necessary than the quality of labour. This was the reason why children above the age of six were engaged as labourers in France (Eli Hecksher, 1935).

According to Giovanni Botero (1558), the strength of a state depends upon two things: increase in population and predominance of industry over agriculture. He also believed that if the resources of production are less and increase in these resources is limited, population should not be more as imbalance between the rate of population and natural resources may invite natural calamities. This thinking of Botero was the main source of inspiration for Malthusian theory (Charles, 1904).

During Mercantilism, increase in population was encouraged. But by the end of this era poverty also increased. From his study of the results of this period, Physiocrats presented another point of view. In the period of mercantilism, agriculture was side lined, but in Physiocratic philosophy, land was given more importance. In their view, land is the basic source of wealth; hence, agricultural activities must be given importance. They also suggested that internal tax reforms must also be given (Encyclopedia Britannica, 1967) due importance along with agriculture. It should be noted that Physiocrats neither theoretically studied population nor had they thought about the problems of over population. Of course, they should not suffer due to increase in population. According to them population increase was only desirable when there was increase in agricultural products.

In Quesney's opinion (1694-1774) population increases parallel to increase in the income of the state. As far as people live happily, increase in population is not a problem. Mirabeau (1715-1789) thought that agriculture should be encouraged, as it is the major source of food (Charles, 1904). In an ideal state population increase is only desirable if resources are adequate. This is the point of view of Mercier de la Riviera. On the other hand, Castilian believed in mercantilism, but still agreed with Physiocrats that land must be given equal importance, as agricultural products are a vital decisive factor for the size of population (UN, 1973).

In the $17^{th}$ and $18^{th}$ centuries, population analyses were based on observations only because of the unavailability of statistical data. But in the $19^{th}$ century population analyses were based on facts, as data were easily available. William Petty's (1968) thoughts on Multiplication of Mankind helped economists of the $19^{th}$ century to understand and explain speculations about population. Montesquien stated that the ancient world was more populous than was the western world of his time. Hume gave reasons for this kind of situation and Robert Wallace (1755) supported Hume. Mr. W. Bail gave the theory of population in which he stated that production increase results in an increase in trade; and this eventually results in increase of population. In Howlet's view increase in population is due to the growth of agriculture.

### 2.3 Malthusian Theory

Population theory was first given by Malthus. He wrote "*an essay on population*" based on a survey that he did in Paris in 1798. He published this essay against the wishes of William Godwin (an English thinker and philosopher) and Marie Jean Antonie Condorcet (a French mathematician, economist and philospher), who were optimistic in their points of view. This essay was titled "*An Essary on the Principle of Population as it Affects the Future Improvement of Society*" (Bealy, 1958). He was afraid of publishing the first book on population. Godwin was an optimistic seer. He believed that the future society will be constituted on the base of humanity and people will wish well of each other. In this society, diseases and wars will be completely eradicated. But the result of Malthus' survey was alarmingly different from Godwin's ideals. Malthus' study revealed that the supply of food grain is not as rapid as increase in population. If this situation prevails it might lead to acute poverty and starvation. His study was based on statistical data. Though he was criticised in the later period, his book is pivotal to the study of population. His successors adopted a more scientific approach in their studies and statement of population theories. But no scholar of population study can neglect Malthus. He holds an important position amongst the population theorists of the world. This is the reason why population theories are divided into the following time-spans: (1) Pre-Malthusian population theories, (2) Malthusian theory of population and (3) Post-Malthusian theories. Post Malthusian theorists are either anti-Malthusian or they are amendments or extension to Malthus' theory (Kenneth Smith, 1951).

Britain was an agricultural country in the $18^{th}$ century. After the first half of this century industrial revolution brought England on the path of rapid progress. But at the same time poverty also increased. Burden of population was increasing day by day. Economic condition of the nation was the principal cause for increase in poverty according to Malthus, while Godwin believed that the poor themselves were responsible for poverty, as they did not desire to free themselves from their prevailing condition. Both these great thinkers never agreed on this issue. Rapid increase in population and economically sick society were responsible for poverty according to Malthusian theory. He also believed that lack of restraint was also one of the principal causes of poverty. His theory emphasizes the importance of food for the human existence. He states: "*First, that food is necessary to the existence of man. Secondly, the passion between the sexes is necessary and will remain nearly in its present state*" (Malthus, 1798). He also prophesied that the law of diminishing returns of agricultural seeds would result in the decrease of agricultural products.

In the improved addition of his book, Malthus has drawn four important measures, which are a landmark of his thinking on population. "*(1) Population is necessarily limited by the means of subsistence (2) population invariably increases where the means of subsistence increase unless presented by some very powerful and obvious checks. (3) These checks and the checks which repress the superior power of population and its effects on a level with the means of subsistence, are all resolvable into moral restraints, vice and misery*" (Malthus, 1798).

In Malthus' view, population will be double in a cycle of every twenty-five years. This increase will be in its geometrical progression, i.e. 1, 2, 4, 8... On the other hand increase in agricultural products will be in arithmetical progression; i.e. 1, 2, 3, 4... Mathus suggested two important measures for population check: (1) preventive check and (2) positive check. Preventive check include abstinence from sex, delay or postponement of marriage, restriction on sexual enjoyment etc. (Mathus, 7$^{th}$ edition, 1872) "*This is the only mode of keeping population on a level with the means of subsistence, which is perfectly consistent with virtue and happiness*" (Kenneth Smith, 1951). Positive measures to check population includes such measures that result in shortening the human longevity. Poverty is the one of the principal positive measures to check population. Apart from this, non-nutritive food, lack of proper clothing, exploitation of labour, seasonal adversities are also important positive measures responsible for population control. Along with these, war and conditions of either draught or excessive rainfall will also play their role in limiting population growth. But in all these positive measures man himself will be the prime victim (David Glass, 1958).

The thinking of Malthus on population gave rise to much discussion on a chain of controversies, which continues. Some thinkers consider Malthus' contribution to population study to be very important while some doubt the originality of his thinking. Criticising Malthus Kaunstsky states: "*His study did no more than to spread the news of what others had discovered*" (David Glass, 1958) because both Machiavelly and Botero – predecessors of Malthus – had already asserted that population increases faster than the increase in the means of livelihood. Thinkers like Francis Bacon, John grant, William Petty, Sir Mathew Hale, Benjamin Franklin, Hume, Robert Wallace, Arthur young, Paley and some of their contemporaries had already expressed almost the similar views (E.P. Hutchinson). Malthus, being their successor, had a chance to study them in details before expressing himself on population. His study of population growth also helped to co-relative economic development with the development of political scenario of that era. Kenneth opines that the ecopolitical scenario of his time provided the right platform to Malthus' theory and political circles accepted it (Kenneth Smith, 1951).

Different scholars have criticized some of Malthus thoughts on population. These are: (1) production of food grains does not increase in proportion with the increase in population, (2) abstinence is the only prevention for population control and (3) increase in population is the sole reason for the increase in poverty. Malthus has also discussed the law of diminishing returns in agricultural production but this can be balanced by increasing productivity in other sectors. His successors also suggested that: (1) instead of abstinence from sex it is better and more practical to use contraceptive methods to control population, (2) increase population is not the only cause of poverty as many more factors are responsible for the increasing poverty in the world. Apart from all these criticisms, his theory is a landmark in population studies. He cannot be neglected while thinking about population problems in the world.

## 2.4 Optimum Theory

According to Malthus, increase in population is a curse, but in optimum theory of population, it is considered bliss in the initial phase of development, provided that it is utilised as a major factor in the production up to the extent that it helps to increase the production up to the maximum limit. After this initial stage increase in population will result in decrease in the per capita income. Prof Cannon (1861-1935) classifies status of population as under population, over population and optimum population. This classification was afterwards named as Optimum Theory of Population. Even before Prof. Cannon established his theory of optimum population, Winkelblack (1810-1865) had already established almost the similar theory (Hutchinson). He had stated that increase in population should be considered normal when production is maximum. Experts like Robertson, Dalton, Carr, Sounders have also explained this theory. These scholars explained the optimum theory of population with reference to maximum population and with reference to maximum per capita income, maximum productivity, economic welfare, normal standard of living, real income and employment (UN, 1973). According to Robins, population is optimum when returns are maximum, while Carr and Sounders attached social welfare with the optimum theory of population. Bolding associated high standard of living with this theory. Thus, the optimum population theory is closely related with socio-economic development.

The increase in population beyond its optimum level is considered as over population. In the initial stage of development maximum utilisation of the means of production is not possible because of less population. With gradual increase in population, there is remarkable increase in labour leading to better utilisation of the means of production. Maximum production is achieved when means of production are utilized to the fullest. Population at this stage is considered optimum, while population before this situation is called less population and after this, it is called over population in general. Total production is lower than optimum when population is either low or high.

Some economists have tried to work out number of the optimum population in their countries. Alfred Sauvey is one of them. In his time, he tried to work out this in numbers and estimated that in his days, between 50 and 75 million of population was optimum population in France (Alfred Sauvey, 1996). Still many experts are of the opinion that finding an exact or even a nearly exact number of optimum population is unrealistic. Alfred Sauvey considered this theory only as a handy tool helpful in explaining the situation of population of a country (Alfred Sauvey, 1966). This theory can be only applied when optimum conditions in all economic sectors prevail. In other words, all factors at their optimum should be applied to understand and explain the concept of optimum population.

## 2.5 Natural Theories (Biological) of Population

These theories explain how natural-biological factors affect population. These theories are based on the fact that the cycle of birth and death is common in all lives; may it be human or animal or vegetation. Various economists have explained the theory of population based on the biological theory of life.

## I. *M.T. Sadler's Density and Fecundity Theory*:

Sadler was Malthus' contemporary but he did not agree with Malthus' theory of population. According to him, the fecundity of human beings is inversely related to the density of population. In his view, population cannot grow at a geometric rate because when population is growing, the density increases, leading to a decline in fecundity. Hence, the population decreases without any conscious attempt on the part of people to do so. According to Sadler, food supply will be increased because of better technologies applied in agriculture parallel to the increase of fecundity of human beings. He derived that when the death rate is high, the birth rate would also be high in order to compensate the death and vice-versa. Sadler in his theory of population found out that "*the fecundity of human beings under similar circumstances varies inversely as their numbers on a given space*" (B.N. Ghosh, 1993).

Pattern of population growth that we see in many of the Asian countries like Japan, China, India, Pakistan etc. show the population growth that prove Salder's theory of population wrong. In these countries density of population does not lead to increased death rate as opined by Sadler. On the contrary, expectation of life has increased in these countries. This means fertility and not fecundity, is a decisive factor in the increase of population.

## II. *Doubleday's Theory of Diet (1790-1870)*

While Salder's population theory is based on the density of population, Doubleday focuses on diet. According to him, "*Increase in population is inversely related to food supply*" (Thompson, 1951). He has shown that fertility decreases when food supply is adequate and it increases when food is scarce. But the condition of adequate food supply is never practically possible. It is always somewhere between scarcity and adequacy. As a result, the rate of fertility is always high. He also believes that fecundity in vegetarians is higher than in the non-vegetarians.

This theory explains relationship between food supply and fertility. However, this theory has not been corroborated (or Substantiated) with facts. Fecundity and fertility are not similar. It cannot be established that the reproductive capacity is more in those who have adequate food. Fertility can be reduced voluntarily. Perhaps Doubleday did not pay attention to this factor when he put forward his theory of population growth.

## III. *Herbert Spencer's Bio-theory*

Herbert Spencer (1867) was a sociologist. He propounded a theory of population in 1852 in which he tried to demonstrate that there is an inverse relationship between complexity of social life and fertility. Increase in complexities of social life results in the decrease in fertility. According to him, in the society engaged in industrial activities, fertility is less than in the society engaged in agricultural activities. This theory falls in the category of natural theory of population because nature affects the reproductive capacity but social complexities need more energy. As a result of this less energy and capacity are left for reproduction. Contrary to this, if social complexities are less, more energy is generated for reproductive act. In a civilized society energy is diverged in various activities leaving less energy for reproduction, hence less children are born resulting in lower population growth. However, this theory does not have adequate empirical evidence. Spencer wanted to explain his theory biologically, so he emphasized various uses of energy. But the problems of population growth are not so simple because numerous factors affect population growth.

### IV. *Gini's Theory*

Gini (1880) discussed a theory of population that explains the social evolution in which the evolution of a nation is closely linked with the changes in the rate of population growth (Thomson, 1951). Gini explains this evolution in three stages: In the initial stage, population growth is very rapid. After this initial rapid growth, the growth rate becomes slow and at last, with the low growth rate the quality of population decreases. In the early stage a nation is simple and undifferentiated in its structure. It has high rate of fertility because people inherit high fertility from their predecessors. With the rapid population growth a complex kind of individual growth happens and simultaneously mercantile growth also takes place. On the other hand, the pressure of population on every field of activity results in war. This marks the beginning of the second stage. In this stage increase in population is not very rapid because strong people are destroyed in war. Population pressure is heavy in the higher strata of society, but this class does not inherit very strong fertility. According to Gini, biological factor is responsible for the decrease in fertility in the second stage of evolution. Fertility is low because fecundity is low. Decrease in population is seen in the higher class of society due to weak fertility but gradually this trait is also observed in all the classes of society. This is because in the due course of time more and more people from the lower class are included in the upper strata. These people now included in the upper class will show the trait of relative sterility. This condition is not a consequence of the social condition, but is the result of the weakening of the reproductive instinct. Thus, biological factor, according to Gini, is responsible for this change. Gini's theory does not consider human-social factor responsible for the changes in population. He gives credit to biological natural forces for the changes in population growth. Nevertheless, natural forces are unknown and humans have no control over them. Gini's theory does not accept the importance of human control over population problem.

V. *Castro's Theory*

Castro (1952) opines that there is a negative relationship between the consumption of protein and fertility. Lavish consumption of proteins results in more fat and less fertility, while less consumption of protein means less fat and high fertility. In the developing countries population growth is rapid because of hunger, i.e. scarcity of food. The state of hunger affects people's levers and their reproductive organs. Less consumption of food devoid of necessary protein makes the workers' levers sluggish. Oestrogen, which is a vital hormone affecting reproductive organs in women is not neutralized in the women of the developing countries because they are not able to consume enough quantity of protein, hence their reproductive capacity is more than the women in the developed countries. According to Castro, this is one of the major reasons of more children in poor population.

Castro's theory cannot be considered as thoroughly scientific because it cannot be proved that the consumption of more protein is the cause of lower fertility. At the same time, it cannot be asserted that hunger will make sex more important. Castro's theory provides only one of the explanations of population growth.

VI. *Net Reproductive Rate Theory (N.R.R.)*

This theory is also known as Kuczynshy's Theory. The difference between birth rate and death rate is not a full proof method to determine the growth rate of population. NRR helps to decide the population growth rate. If NRR=1, the rate of population growth remains static. The geometrical ratio of the would be mothers in future must be NRR=1. To decide this ratio it is necessary to find out the number of women in the high reproductive age groups; i.e. between 15 and 45. But this alone is not enough. The number of women who are either unmarried or widows, or unwilling to give birth, or dead, must also be deducted from the total number of women in the above stated age group. The ratio of net number of child bearing women (future mothers) to the total number of child bearing women (present mothers) help to measure the growth rate of population, known as the Net Reproductive Rate – NRR.

This is one of the important theories in the study of the rate of population growth. It helps to differentiate between fertility and fecundity. Even if fecundity is high fertility can be low. This theory only studies the quantitative aspect of biological population growth. This theory is one-sided, as it does not take into account the socio-economical and institutional aspects responsible for population growth.

### VII. *Pearl's Logistic Curve Theory*

The population theory given by Raymond Pearl in 1925 and known as Pearl's Logistic Curve Theory which explains that population growth is cyclic. According to his theory, population growth is rapid in the beginning but after the initial rapid growth, it remains stagnant and then the growth rate decreases. At the completion of this cyclic process, again population growth becomes rapid. He came to this conclusion from his study of the population growth pattern in France, Germany and the USA. Pearl does not fully agree with Malthus. He asserts that population not only increases rapidly as asserted by Malthus, but it also increases at the end part of the cyclical change. This theory did not gain much importance.

## 2.6 Karl Marx's Relative Surplus Population Theory

Karl Marx (1867-1959) has no direct contribution in population theory but in his 'Das Capital', he points out two important things regarding population (Karl Marx, Das Capital Vol.1, 1867). (1) He strongly criticizes Malthusian theory of population by asserting that Mathus' theory cannot be scientifically explained. Marx further remarks: "*His work in first form, was nothing more than schoolboyish, superficial and parsonic declamatory from Defoe, Sir James Stuart, Townsend, Fromblin, Wallace and others; did not contain a single sentence throughout by Malthus himself*" (Karl Marx, Das Capital Vol.1, 1867). (2) Marx also shows his concern for population problems which emerged alongwith and due to progress of capitalism in the world. The emergence of capitalism and socialism put capital and labour against each other. Constant increase in capital against labour created problems of unemployment. This in turn resulted in the problem of over population. Marx does not consider this growth as a natural consequence. On the contrary, he was of the opinion that the replacement of capital in the place of labour and its consequential unemployment was responsible for the problem of over population. In his view, population theories can be considered only on the basis of the pattern of production of a given period. If population theories are based on history, they are valid only during the said historic period.

While capitalists consider high fertility as one of the major factors responsible for population growth, Marx does not consider this factor very important in population growth. He looks at the problem of population growth from an altogether different perspective. According to him, labourers are always a soft target for all kind of exploitation: (1) Compared to their productivity they are under paid. (2) Machines replace the work force. These two factors are responsible for the creation of a group of labourers who are unable to look after their children due to poverty. As a result of this, in long run, the problem of relative surplus population becomes graver. In capitalism, labourers work harder and harder to create more capital; but unfortunately, at the end of this cycle they themselves become the victims of unemployment.

Surplus labour is both reason and result of capitalism, hence it is an unavoidable problem of capitalism; (V.I. Lenin, 1941) and especially when production is an unorganised activity, surplus labour is even a more serious problem. We need not go far back in the history to find an example of this. In the time of the great depression in the nineteen thirties comprehensive unemployment was created mainly due to unorganised production system. According to Lenin, the study of surplus labour with reference to human reproduction rate is never given due consideration in capitalistic thinking. On the contrary, the study of the said problem is based on the theory related to capitalism (V.I. Lenin, 1934). Population related changes such as mortality, population migration, birth rate, etc. are not related to the demand of labour. Surplus labours then tend more towards agriculture, gradually increasing load of population burden on agriculture. This in turn results in imbalanced distribution of population in economic sector.

Marx divides surplus labour in three categories:

(1) Floating category, i.e. surplus labour due to the use of machinery.

(2) Latent category which includes surplus labour engaged in agriculture.

(3) Stagnant category inclusive of the exploited class of labour suffering from irregular employment opportunities.

In socialism surplus labour is not a problem because production is a co-operative activity. Socialists believe that this is basically a problem created by capitalistic society because in such a society, production is an activity undertaken for earning more profits based on individual efforts. Not only this, but also more and more capital alongwith the use of sophisticated high-tech machinery have made the problem of surplus labour graver.

Marx's views on the problem of population are based on his thinking on capitalism, hence, his theory can be considered as the theory of surplus labour and not as the theory of relative surplus population. Marx did not discuss population related changes in this theory, but he only kept in mind the method of production in a capitalist society.

Karl Marx's this point of view has been proven wrong in the country like the U.S.A. Due to the development of export based industries the demand of labour has increased greatly. This proves that capital and labour are not competitors but complimentary to each other Karl Marx's line of thinking is lop-sided as it is purely based on his criticism of capitalism.

### 2.7 Dumant's Theory of Social Capillarity

The population theory given by Dumant (1890) is known as the theory of social capillarity. The principle of capillarity is very important in society. According to him, Malthusian theory of population has proved to be wrong (Thompson, 1951). It is applicable only in an uncivilized society where population increases in geometrical progression like it happens in animals. In the initial stage of civilization there is co-relation between availability of food and population growth. According to Dumant, in a fully civilized society the theory of social capillarity is applicable. Human beings at this stage of civilization try to achieve both name and fame where children are a major hindrance to their progress. Hence small family size is desirable to achieve social status. As income of a family increases, the number of children decreases due to social capillarity. "*Just as a column of liquid must be thing in order to rise under the force of capillarity so must be a family be small to rise in the social scale*" (A. Dumant, 1870). This is the reason why birth rate is low in cities, while in rural area birth rate is high. High standard of living, high income and wealth, ambition and development oriented thinking, more knowledge, social status, etc. are responsible for low birth rate in the urban area, while villages show a totally opposite scenario, hence, high birth rate. In a socialist society, birth rate is high. As socialism offers equal opportunities to all, destruction of social capillarity happens. This leads to high birth rate. Contrary to this, capitalism does not offer equal opportunities to all, hence high birth rate.

Dumant's Theory does not clarify as to what type of capillarity he favours. His idea of social capillarity is rather vague. If money, income of manpower is the capillarity, high birth rate may be favoured. It cannot be generalised that birth rate in urban areas is always low because majority of the urban population is migrated from elsewhere. Secondly, it is not mandatory to lower birth rate to acquire higher social status. It has been observed that generally economic, social and political factors also play an important role in securing higher social status.

### 2.8 Mal-adjustment Theory

The population theory of American economist and welknown social reformer, Henry George is known as the social Maladjustment theory

(Thompson, 1951). Explaining his theory George states: "*Law of population accords with and is subordinate to the law of intellectual developments and any danger that human beings may have brought into a world where they cannot be provided for, arises not from the ordinances of nature but from the social maladjustment that in the midst of wealth condemn men to want*" (Henry George, 1905). Like Spencer, he also believed that intellectual progress of human beings lead to lower birth rate. He considered feudal system responsible for high birth rate. He favoured that with the eradication of landlordism, small land-tillers or marginal farmers will become landowners and production of food grain will go high. This will help to solve problems of high population. But his theory does not make it clear as to how intellectual development of the population will automatically lead to low birth rate. He does not specify if decrease in birth rate is due to lower fertility or because of the adoption of family planning by the population. What kind of social maladjustment is responsible for high population is not very clearly stated in his theory.

## 2.9 F.S. Nitti's Principle of Individuality

Nitti (1894) opined that increase in population is always not desirable because in certain situations population growth is an important factor in the development of civilisation. If population growth and the development of an individual happen simultaneously, population problems do not rise. Economic, social and biological factors play an important role in population growth. Also, less important or secondary factors like psychological, political and social ethics are responsible for population growth. According to Nitti, economic and biological factors are the most crucial among these (F.S. Nitti, 1894). He also believed that when individual's progress will take place in the society, the inequality of wealth would be reduced. This in turn will lead to social co-operation; and in this situation, population will not increase at a rate more than the rate of increase in food supply. Nitti strongly asserts that economic and biological factors affect population growth but he fails to clarify as to how these factors play their role. On the one hand, he gives importance to economic factors, while on the other hand he states that economists can hardly solve the population problems. He has not even clarified how biological theory can help to solve the population problems. He also accepts the growth of an individual and eradication of inequality as factors responsible for low birth rate but again fails to clarify how all these will work in solving the problems of population.

### 2.10 Ungern Sternberg's Theory of Rationalism

Ungern Sternberg (1931) connects fertility not merely with biological factors but also with psychological factor. He affirms that material wealth in itself is not responsible for decline in fertility rate. He also opines that poverty cannot be considered directly responsible for high fertility rate. He observes that it is not necessary that fertility rate would be lower in villages as compared to towns and cities. He believes that rational thinking is required to lower the rate of birth. Economic development lowers fertility but it is also equally true that economic development can only take place as and when population growth declines. "*One limits the number of births in order to be able to obtain prosperity. Prosperity, therefore, is not the cause but the goal, and birth control the means for the attainment of this goal*" (Ungern Sternberg, 1931).

Capitalistic thinking helps to lower the rate of fertility according to him. People want to gain economic, social, political power, prestige and possession. To gain these, their decisions need to be governed by self-interest. Hence, all their activities are guided by their desires. They try to remove obstacles hindering their progress. This mentality is seen in both men and women. Women also desire to attain equal status in society as well as in their professional career. Therefore, both men and women think twice before they decide to produce children.

Thus rational psychological thinking affects fertility. Ungern Sternberg overlooks other factors affecting fertility in his theory of population. The process of urbanization exerts additional economic pressure. People cannot afford a large family. Urbanization thus reduces fertility. Prosperity, as Ungern Sternberg suggests in his theory, is not only the goal but also the cause of decline in fertility. This has been found in the study of the population growth in many countries.

## 2.11 Frank Fetter's Theory of Voluntarism

In the opinion of Frank Fetter (1894), fertility is low in rich class. He gives reasons for this: (1) The cost of child rearing is very high in rich class. Moreover, children become earning members at a late age. (2) The rich people want to enjoy life without hindrance of children. (3) They do not want that their property is sub-divided into smaller parts. The rate of fertility is high in the poor class, for the following reasons: (1) The cost of child rearing is very low. (2) Their children become earning members at a very young age, and (3) they do not think much about the future. They are ignorant and illiterate and they do not have to worry about the problems of heredity, as there is hardly anything to inherit from their parents. He believes that birth rate would fall as a result of economic development. He also believed that in socialism there is no such incentive, which would cause reduction in the rate of birth.

Frank Fetter comes to the conclusion that in rich class family size is smaller than in poor class as they give birth to lesser number of children they actually desire. However, this is not always found true. It is not necessary that every rich family will have smaller number of children. His opinion that socialism does not provide any incentive to decrease the birth rate is not also acceptable. Birth rate would automatically decline when the standard living would be better.

### 2.12 L. Brento's Theory of Increasing Prosperity and Pleasure

According to L. Brento, the principal objective of human life is to achieve material prosperity and to derive pleasure out of it. Therefore, rich people have various means of obtaining pleasure. They are able to buy means of recreation and pleasure. They also get satisfaction from the fields of industry trade and commerce, with the help of advanced technologies. They do not only rely upon sexual pleasure, hence, birth rate is low in richer class. The poor have only one alternative to obtain pleasure; i.e. sex. They do not have energy, money or time to obtain other means of enjoyment and recreation. At the end of a hectic day, sex is the only easily available mean of pleasure for them. Therefore, birth rate is high in the poor class.

L. Brento's theory gives an impression that the rich enjoy less sex than the poor, but this is not true. The rich are more careful, therefore they can take precautions to keep the birth rate low, while lack of privacy and due to physical exhaustion the poor cannot involve themselves in sexual activities as often as the rich can. The birth rate among the poor is high because they are either ignorant about the contraceptive methods or they cannot afford to take such precautions. This means birth rate is not only influenced by sex, poverty or prosperity, but also by many other socio-cultural, economic and psychological factors.

***Arthur T. Hadley's Intelligence Prudence and Control Theory of Populations***

Hadley correlates low birth rate and happy life in his theory of population. He opines that prudent people enjoy a happy life and practice family planning. Individual's ambitions and desire to succeed in all walks of life are also vital factors responsible for the reduction of birth rate. He states, "*Intellectual man is more capable of birth control than emotional person. He can exercise more self-restraint*" (T. H. Arthur, 1896).

Hadley's theory falls short in satisfactorily explaining the process of birth rate and its role in population growth, as the complex factor like birth rate cannot be properly explained only by his intelligence and prudence theory. It is untrue to say that poor people are not happy and only the prudent and the intelligent people enjoy happy life. Even poor people with high rate of birth can also live a happy life in their own way, as happiness basically is a state of mind and it has nothing to do either with intelligence or with worldly riches.

## 2.13 Economic Theories of Population

### I. *Leibenstein's Economic Theory of Population*

Prof. Leibenstein's (1974) population theory asserts that changes in population are determined by various external factors. It is not possible to separate demographic factors from other factors. His theory also points out that demographic factors cannot be ignored in considering economic problems (H. Leibenstein, 1974). In his view, population growth is an obstacle to economic growth especially in densely populated countries. If other factors remain the same, increase in population reduces per capita income. However, any factor responsible in increasing income will initially increase the rate of population growth. Reduction in population growth can be explained by changes in per capita income. On the other hand, chemical and medical discoveries also help to reduce mortality.

Increase in average income increases population in economically backward countries but not in advanced countries. On the other hand, mortality declines due to better medical facilities and awareness of public health. However, fertility rate remains almost constant, hence, population grows. Tradition, culture, people's attitudes and social environment are responsible for this trend. In the early stage of development, according to Prof. H. Leibenstein, population theory can be attached with and explained through the theories of economic development. He believes that without economic development birth rate cannot decline. This means economic development is the pre-condition for the decline in birth rate.

Further, Leibenstein states that an adequate theory of population should be able to explain the changes in demographic factors during the process of development. Thomson, Backer, Laundry and others have explained this in their theories of demographic transition. However, their theories are based on a broad scale and provide historical generalization. Thus, transition theory does not explain any critical problem concerned with economic development and population. It falls short in explaining the differences in per capita income and the nature of population problems.

Laibenstein's theory goes one step further. According to him, neither high density of population is an obstacle in economic development nor low density of population helpful in economic development. Economic development in his view depends upon the optimum use of natural resources along with capital endowment and better technology. He points out that decrease in population growth and economic development are interdependent. At the same time, he also states that economic development is pre-condition for decline in population growth.

Leibenstein's theory explains the reasons for decline in fertility. The factors determining mortality are well known. Mortality declines with increase in income because income affects the standard of life. Family size depends upon motivation. With the increase in income, knowledge of family planning also becomes better. However, people in the underdeveloped countries neither have adequate knowledge of contraceptive methods, nor do they have means to use such methods. Economic development also spreads rationality and information related to family planning. These factors are the determinants of fertility trends. However, the lack of motivation related to population problems in backward countries cannot be explained.

Leibenstein also explains an economic theory of population in terms of utility and cost. According to him, birth of a child in a family involves two types of costs: direct cost and indirect cost. The direct cost includes cost of food, clothing, medicine, education etc. The indirect costs are opportunities and income parents have to forego due to the addition of a child in the family. Three main changes occur because of economic development with reference to cost. These are known as *survival effects, income effects and occupation* distribution effects.

As income of a family increases, the development is boosted, but side-by-side the cost of child rearing also increases. With the birth of every child, marginal utility decreases. Of course, the consumption, utility of a child, i.e. social status, personal satisfaction etc., remain the same. Survival rates raise the utility curves but the survival effects are not in proportion to increase in survival rates. The increase in the survival years also increase the productive value of each additional child, however, increased survival in children in the higher age groups is unimportant to the parents because the mature children will have their own family burdens; and parents will have to give up the hopes of their children being of any use in their old age. This is the reason why after a certain point survival effect becomes weak and parents give up the desire to add any more children to their family. The occupational distribution effects relate to the increase in the cost of child rearing. With the increase in income specialization and mobility also increases. Opportunities for the child labour become limited. On the other hand, education training becomes expensive. In such conditions if the size of a family is small, parents can avail of the new and better economic opportunities. The more rapid rate of growth, the greater is the desire for small family. Leibenstein has found correlation between per capita income and population growth: (1) When income is low, mortality is high; and because death rate is high, birth rate has to be high. The utility from the marginal child is very high but the cost of rearing a marginal child is low. According to Leibenstein, in the transitional period of economic development, income increases and death rate decreases but fertility does not decreases immediately; because reproductive age increases, and people do not immediately become aware of the fact that mortality has decreased. (2) Gradually, as income increases, more children survive and the utility of a child as a source of income declines. On the other hand, both money and opportunity cost of a child rearing increases and fertility tends to decline.

With the increase in income, the gap between fertility and mortality also declines gradually. This stimulates sustained economic development.

In Leibenstein's theory, per capita income is a positive factor of population growth related to various stages of economic development. Hence, the rate of population growth can only be checked if efforts are made to raise per capita income at a necessary minimum size.

According to him, population increases with the increase in income to a certain level because mortality declines along with increase in income. At the same time, fertility declines with increase in income, hence, birth rate declines; but the rate of mortality declines even faster, resulting in the increase in population. In the developing countries decline in population is not only due to increase in per capita income but also socio-cultural changes, aptitudes and outlook of the people, education and intellectual perception of the people play a vital role. Leinbenstein overlooks the role of the state in reducing the population growth rate. It is not advisable to wait for increase in per capita income as a necessary tool to check population growth because this attitude might result in population explosion. The Measures taken by the state towards family planning prove more fruitful towards achieving control over population growth.

In a backward country where resources are utilized in a limited way, per capita income cannot be increased unless steps are taken to check population growth, hence Leinbenstein's theory advocating economic development first and then population control seems not very feasible. However, he does provide us with a theory of population based on economic development, which can be used in context of development planning.

### II. *Gary Becker's Economic Analysis of Fertility Theory*

A theory of fertility that has attracted considerable attention in recent years was given by Gary Becker (1960). His theory is also known as Chicago School Theory of Fertility as he belonged to the University of Chicago. His disciples have also contributed a great deal in the post Becker research on population theory. He presented a micro economic model of fertility to explain his theory. Micro economic theory explains the demand for and supply of consumer durable goods. In the same of way, Becker's fertility theory explains how parents decide family size with reference to number and quality of children. His theory also explains economic analysis for high or low fertility.

Individual experiences are used as determining factors in formulating Becker's theory of fertility. He assumes that fertility behaviour of parents depends on economic considerations and that income level and fertility level are positively correlated with increase in income. Parents will desire to have more children. However at the same time it has been observed that individuals with higher income desire less children because they want higher quality children in terms of education, health, intelligence etc., therefore, having more children is an expensive proposition. The '*price effect*' of higher quality children is more important than the '*income effect*' according to the model given by Becker.

His theory is based on the principles of demand and supply. Demand for children is based on the income of the family and the cost of a child. If the cost of child rearing is high, the demand for a child will be low. Even when income increases, parents show preference for child quality and not for child quantity. The price of a child also includes the loss of that extra income that a mother loses during the time of pregnancy and delivery. This monetary loss is quite considerable; hence mother is not ready to lose that income. This also is a reason why the number of children in a high income family remains low.

Becker tried to study the reasons of diverse fertility rate in the various income group people of the USA and came to the conclusion that the decision of parents about having children commensurate with their decision of the purchase of commodities. But children are not like commodity preferences that is why with increase in income parents' demand for children will also increase. Contrary to this, they expect more satisfaction from every additional child. Utility derived from them should be more than the expenditure on child-rearing. This utility of children depends upon quality of children. The birth of a child is full of uncertainties. The uncertainty causes divergence between the actual fertility and the desired fertility hence parents try to maximize the total satisfaction. The expenditure on a child according to Becker includes both monetary cost and the loss of time. He observed that the satisfaction derived from children is based on both quality and quantity of children.

Becker then emphasizes the parents' aspiration of their children's standard of living as the effective cost of children. Therefore, the more the cost of children, the less the demand for children. This is the reason why parents opt for quality of children they want, and this in turn determines the expenditure per child. If the expenditure is more, the quality of children will be better and the satisfaction derived from them will be greater. Becker made two important contributions in the study of the relationship between child quality and child quantity. He made his first study in 1960 in which he presented his thoughts on quantity of children, and in 1973 he attempted to study the quality of children jointly with Levis (G. Becker, H. Levis, 1973).

The demand of child quantity and quality are affected by changes in income. In his article with Levis (1973) he tried to study the effect of children income on the price of children. In his first article (1960) he pointed out that the quality of children is directly related to the expenditure voluntarily made by parents above a certain required minimum. These criteria also help to decide family size. However, Becker agrees that expenditure only does not decide the quality of a child. There are many more factors responsible in deciding the quality of a child, over which parents hold least control. Income is a very decisive factor of fertility. As parents' income increases, they want to spend more on each child, therefore, when income is high, expenditure is even higher; and demand for children is less.

According to Becker when expenditure is more in maintaining a child's quality; i.e. the child price in this relation, fertility declines. It becomes necessary to study the cost of child's quality otherwise as income increases, both demand and quality of children will increase. As Becker's model shows, the size of family is decided by the satisfaction the parents get from their children against the child price. It can be derived that with the increase in income both quality and quantity of children increase.

Becker explained the negative relationship between fertility and income neither in terms of price effect nor in terms of the negative income elasticity of the demand for children, but in the inverse relationship between the ability to control; both income and fertility.

Becker's model gives us a concept of child's quality, but fails to suggest the measures to maintain this quality. Boom Turchi has rejected Becker's concept of quality as an unreal concept (1973). It is not possible to calculate the utility derived from a child in the same way as it can be calculated from consumer goods. It is also not possible to calculate the opportunity cost of a child. Education also plays an important role on the quality of a child. In some countries education is provided either at subsidized rate or free. Therefore, it cannot be proved that with the rise in income child price will also increase considerably. Becker compared the demand of a child with the demand of consumer goods. This is not empirically true. Leibenstein's explanation based on price–effect is an insufficient explanation. Becker also argues that people in the higher income group have less number of children because in society employed mothers with very high income are not ready to sacrifice their time and income for child birth and child care. However his arguments also falls short as such mothers can hire caretaker to look after their children. Thus, Becker's model is full of loopholes, hence insufficient to explain the relationship between income, child price and fertility.

### III. *Easterline's Relative Income Hypothesis of Fertility*

Richard Easterline (1969) was Becker's contemporary and agreed with Becker's assumptions regarding fertility. Easterline emphasized the importance of economic factor in population growth. He also considered social factors to provide an adequate explanation of human fertility behaviour. According him fertility behaviour is influenced by expectations and the resources available to the individuals to fulfill these expectations, hence it is not the absolute income, but related to these expectations, which is responsible for their particular fertility behaviour. His theory is known as the relative income theory of fertility.

According to his theory, Parents' aspiration depends upon their standard of living and they tend to consider their relative income before thinking of an additional child in the family. Economic and social factors influence their fertility behaviour.

There are some noticeable similarities as well as differences between the theories of Becker and Easterline. The differences are quite striking. (1) Becker opines that the tastes of parents remain constant while in Easterline's view they do not but go on changing with socialization. (2) According to Becker, prices are independent of domestic consumptions, while Easterline believes that prices are not independent. (3) Becker explains that fertility behaviour is based on purely economic factors, while Easterline considers social factors as equally important decisive factors in explaining fertility behvaiour of people. In Becker's opinion, parents think about the future standard of living of the children before deciding about an additional child, while Easterline opines that parents think about their own standard of living, and not about their children's standard of living while considering about an additional child in the family.

*Both Becker and Easterline believe that fertility is positively related* with income. As both of them belong to the modern school of economists, it becomes important to study their opinions as regards the relationship between income and fertility. Easterline's explanation of the inverse relationship between income and fertility is clearer than that of Gery Becker's.

According to Easterline the balance between parents' income and their aspirations is basically important in deciding fertility level. Even when the income of parents is high but the aspiration level is low, the number of children will be more. But when both income and aspiration levels are high parents do not desire an additional child because in that case they find it difficult to maintain both their standard of living and provide their children with necessary amenities. Parents are always worried about the maintenance of their standard of living, hence if income level is low, they would not desire for an additional child. When newly married couples inherit a high standard of living from parents they try to maintain the same high level. Their aspiration level is high; hence even with the rise in income they try to maintain the level of their aspiration and desire less children. Adequate income is the pre-condition for such behaviour. Thus, the balance between earning and pattern of consumption of the young couples has a decisive influence on their fertility behaviour.

Easterline does not overlook other factors affecting the fertility trend of humans. Like Becker he also talks about opportunity cost, but in an indirect manner. He agrees that employment of women affects fertility behaviour of couples because when mother is employed the couple has to spend more on child rearing. The use of contraceptive methods also plays a role in deciding fertility behaviour. However, the most important trend in fertility behaviour according to Easterline is the balance between the levels of aspiration, i.e. tastes and preferences of parents, and the level of their income.

Easterline emphasizes that the decision made by one generation to have children influences the supply of labour force in the successive generation. Moreover, the tastes and preferences of the previous generation determine the consumption pattern of the next generation. These effects create cyclic forces. Easterline's explanation for the population explosion in the USA after World War-II is based on this belief. Ghosh terms this concept as Inter-generational Echo Effects (1993).

According to Easterline, family background is important for the preferences of young parents, but in fact, many more factors are responsible for the aspirations of the younger generation. Many of them are unable to attain their aspiration level set by themselves still they desire additional children. The birth of an additional child obviously does not depend upon the calculations of parents, because it is not possible to estimate the possible cost benefit of the prospective child at the time of conception. Moreover, employment of women also considerably affects the fertility behaviour. The loss of future income and time due to childbirth and postnatal care may reduce fertility. The effects of socialization also do not permit parents to have large number of children because the monetary burden of additional children would push them at the bottom level of social capillarity. Both aspiration and relative income are important factors in deciding fertility, but there are no set criteria to calculate precisely when the level of income and the level of aspiration become volatile in the context of economic growth. Therefore, the concept of permanent income–which is more stable income–may prove more useful in deciding fertility behaviour of the individuals than the concept of Easterline's relative income.

### 2.14 Summary

In ancient times, thinking on population was limited to the sphere of philosophy but in modern time the field of demographic studies cover the problems of population and includes all qualitative, quantitative and human welfare aspects. Researches are being taken up to find out reasons of various demographic changes taking place all over the world and also, to find reasons and suitable solutions for population explosion in different parts of the world.

Greek thinkers and philosophers like Plato and Aristotle had thought about the optimum size of population for an ideal state. However, in their thinking population was taken not as a problem, but in their philosophy the size of population depended upon the size and requirements of the state. In the medieval period, European thinkers favoured the growth of population because that was the time when trade and commerce flourished between the countries of Europe and Asia. Their thinking was based on mercantilism and political economy. There thinking was lop – sided because they did not consider the complete dynamics of population growth from the point of view of human welfare. They advocated population growth because labour force was needed to increase the income and wealth of the state, hence they did not think about per capita income and monetary conditions of individuals. Nevertheless this medieval thinking could not gain ground for a long time, as the British, French and Italian thinkers in the mid $18^{th}$ century rejected the mercantilism of their predecessors based purely on economic grounds. They brought in the concept of the dependence of population upon the means of subsistence.

In the time span between $15^{th}$ and $18^{th}$ centuries various philosophical assumptions and thinking on population took place. Population theories were shaped and re-shaped by various thinkers, especially in Europe, population specific studies were undertaken. Grant (1662) was one such thinker of the $17^{th}$ century who conducted statistical study of mortality in Britain. His paper entitled '*Natural and Political Observation on the Bills of Mortality*' was an interesting study on the population of the London city.

Among the anti-mercantilist thinkers, Malthus' views on population are of vital importance. His thinking has been both appreciated and criticized by his contemporaries as well as his successors until to day. Malthus wrote his essay "*The Principles of Population*" criticizing the medieval mercantilism. He edited his essay thrice. In the third edition, he wrote that population is checked by the means of subsistence, and that population invariably increases if means of subsistence increase; unless it is prevented from growing by '*some very powerful and obvious checks*'. Malthus and other $18^{th}$ century thinkers had rationalistic approach towards the study of population theories. They also thought about socio-economic implications of population growth and considered human institutions as instrumental in the cycle of the natural order of birth and death. Thinkers like Condorcet and Godwin differed on the issue of the character of the '*natural order*'. They thought that the natural society was one in which natural resources should be held common, and eventually progress of the human species would continue. Malthus had rejected the views of Condorcet and Godwin. In his essay, he analyzed the reasons of dire poverty. According to him, increase in the means of subsistence is the cause of increase in population, unless there is some powerful check on population growth. Malthus discussed three basic concepts in his theory of population: (1) Production of food increase in arithmetical progression. (2) Population increases in geometrical progression. (3) Positive and preventive checks are necessary for population control. However, he had no faith in the effectiveness of preventive checks because abstinence is almost impossible, hence positive checks are more important. These include natural calamities, wars, epidemics etc. Malthus was the first thinker to give a comprehensive theory based on eco-condition.

In the first half of the 19th century, the population theories evolved in two opposite directions: The population theories propounded in this period were either pro-Malthusian or anti-Malthusian. Karl Marx was one of those who rejected Malthusian theory of population and gave an alternate population theory that is known as Relative Surplus Population Theory. In this theory, he discussed the reasons for over population and considered capitalism as one of the major factors responsible for over population. Cannon and his associates gave another population theory that is known as Optimum Theory of Population. This was also not in line of Malthus. This theory does not consider population growth as a curse, if it does not affect maximum per capita income. This theory analyses under population, optimum population and over population on the basis of economic factors affecting population growth.

The Transition Theories of Population given by Thompson, Warren, E.W. Notestein and Blacker explain the relationship between population growth and economic development. These theories explain the changes in birth and death rates in the various stages of economic development. Death rate decreases rapidly as a result of economic development but birth rate does not decrease so rapidly. Social development is a necessary pre-condition to bring about decrease in birth rate. Social development is a long-term process; hence in the initial stage of development the gap between birth rate and death rate is wide. Along with the economic development, both qualitative and quantitative changes take place in population, but it is a long-term process, hence the quick decrease in death rate causes population explosion. Urbanisation is also a necessary change that takes place due to economic development causing reduction in birth rate. It has long-term social impacts in which small family size, better education, more expenditure on child-rearing etc. are the unavoidable social changes of economic development.

The modern population theories of Leibenstein, Becker and Easterline are based on economic variables. These theories explain and discuss variations in fertility trends from an altogether different perspective. According to them the demand for and supply of children and economic development are strongly interrelated. They take into consideration income effect, cost effect, opportunity cost, direct and indirect cost, etc. as important factors affecting population growth.

The population theories that are given by socialists, economists and demographers cover a long period from Plato-Aristotle to modern day thinkers and population experts. An overview of these theories provide an interesting insight into the evolution of the theories and also show the changes that have taken place in the thinking of the people during this long time span.

# CHAPTER – III

# SOCIO-ECONOMIC CHARACTERISTICS AND DEMOGRAPHIC PROFILE

## 3.1 Population Growth

Socio-economic and demographic characteristics are interrelated. There are constant changes in these factors, and these changes affect socio-economic development and population growth. This chapter attempts to discuss socio-economic characteristics and demographic profile with reference to India, Gujarat and Surat.

Economic development is reflected in the standard of living of the population. Hence it is necessary to study the structure of population, social development and social changes, as these are both cause and effect of the economic development of a country. The structure of population includes demographic changes like growth of population, changes in the density of population and proportion of work force in the total population. The study of the changes in the above-cited aspects are important in the study of economic development. Educational awareness is another important feature of the social changes of a country. Literacy rate increases economic development and vice-versa. Health is also another important feature of social development. Better health brings down the infant mortality rate and increases life expectancy which creates a healthy society. All these social changes affect economic development Changes in the traditional structure of a society are also important in the study of economic development. Amitabh Shukla (1995) observes, ".... *the population and its characteristics closely influence the process and level of economic development, these factors are affected by each of them. Population and its demographic features are mainly responsible for development or under-development of any region or country.*" It has been observed that economic development is rapid in those countries where the relationship of economic resources is favourable or is changing for the better. Socio-economic changes are also studied from the perspective of poverty in a society. As structural changes take place, industrial sector gains importance and it may alter the pace of economic development. As a result of this, occupational re-distribution also takes place and population burden is transferred from agricultural sector to industrial sector. GNP and GNP per capita, the major indicators of economic development, are closely related to population growth, as stated before. The reports of census, being conducted in India at regular intervals of every ten years, are the main source of the demographic information.

India is one of the developing countries of the world. The general trends of population indicate that population growth in the developing countries is more rapid than in the developed countries, which adversely affects economic development. At present India stands second to China in population growth. The steady decline in population growth in China is a clear indicator that in near future India will surpass China in population and will be the world's highest populous country. This serious matter might greatly affect India's programmes for economic development.

According to 2001 census, the population of India is 1,027,015247 (Provisional Population Totals, Paper-II), but by the year 2016 it will be 126.4 crores. This information indicates that the family planning and other programmes conducted by the Government machinery and NGOs for public awareness have not gained satisfactory success in India.

India possesses about 2.4 per cent of the world's land area and 14.6 per cent of the total of the world's population. The land area of India is 324 million square kilometers. The present population exceeds the combined population of the USA and all the Republics of Russia. In contrast to India, these countries together cover about 21.3 per cent of the world's land area and share nearly 40 per cent of the world's income and support only 12 per cent of the world's total population. At present the rate of population growth in India is estimated to 2.2 per cent per year. Sixteen million of population is added every year. This large addition is one of the major factors obstructing the socio-economic development of India.

Kingsley Denis' (1951) observation provides an interesting insight in understanding the trends of India's population growth. According to his estimates, from 300 B.C. to 1700 A.D. the population growth in India remained steady at 125 million. The main reason for the zero growth was the existence of high birth rate and high death rate, due to various reasons. With the establishment of the British rule and the restoration of internal peace and better health and medical services the erstwhile steady growth rate of population began to increase at a steady pace. This trend totally changed the socio-economic scenario of India.

The present scene of India's population growth is full of diversities and peculiarities. These diversities are based on religion, education, family type and other social differences. There are also economic diversities, which are based on occupational distribution of population, problems of inter-state population migration and population migration from rural to urban sectors. The peculiarities of population in India can be classified as under: (i) low age at marriage, (ii) large family size, (iii) traditional concept of family, (iv) low literacy rate, (v) high mortality rate, (vi) low standard of living and (vii) insufficient or meager health care services.

The major problems India is facing to day regarding her population are, (i) large size of population and (ii) rapid population growth. These have posed difficulties in the way of the economic development of the country. Hence, it is necessary to dilate upon this growth, its causes and interpret the growth trends in terms of the most acceptable formulation about population; i.e. the theory of demographic transition.

According to the census report the rapid increase in population in India started in 1921 and it has been very rapid since 1951. This growth is so serious that it has been described as population explosion.

From the table - 3.1 it is observed that there is a continuous increase in population except for a short period between 1901 and 1921. During the twenty years between 1901 and 1921, this increase was of the order of about 129 lakh. This works out to be a little more than six lakh or 0.27 per cent annually. Before 1921 the rise in population was slow but after 1921 there was a rapid and uninterrupted increase in population. This is the reason why the 1921 is described as the year of the 'great divide'. Despite the Second World War and the famine and the partition of India, the decade 1941-51 witnessed a huge rise of 424 lakh in population. The annual growth rate which was under one per cent before 1921 and just above one per cent till 1951, more than doubled, to over two per cent. This growth rate far exceeds the rate of growth of several countries. During this period the growth rate in countries like China and Sri Lanka is half than that of India, i.e. about one per cent, while in the developed countries like U.K., USA, Japan, etc. the growth rate is even much less than one per cent.

The growth rate of population in India shows a clear dividing line. Between 1901 and 1951 the growth rate of population was very rapid. After 1951 the population growth rate becomes more rapid.

The population explosion in India has seriously aggravated the problem of economic development. Our Government authority – both at the state level and central level – planners and non-Government organizations are making efforts to raise the standard of living of people but high birth rate and low death rate are the two major obstacles in the path of progress. Birth rate, death rate and population migration are the three major determinants of population growth. First two determinants are natural and the third one is not a factor actually affecting population growth, but it affects the redistribution of population.

If birth rate is greater than death rate, population increases and if death rate is greater than birth rate, population decreases. Consequently, the differential movement in these two rates can provide an explanation of the patterns of population growth. The trends in birth and death rates in India are given in table - 3.2.

As shown in table - 3.2 both birth rate and death rate were high up to 1921, which was the reason of low growth rate of population. After this death rate rapidly declined compared to birthrate. But up to 1950 the difference between birth rate and death rate was not very high. After 1951 death rate, rapidly went down compared to birthrate, which resulted in a big difference between the two. Consequently, population growth became more rapid. This trend of population growth is seen up to 1981. Regarding this trend in India Agarwal (1991) observes, "*The birth rate in India was 37 per thousand in 1981. It is about 31 at present (1991). Compared to birthrate in many countries, this is very high. For instance, according to the 1991 statistics, the birth rate is 10 for Germany, 10 for Japan, 14 for the U.K. and 14 for Sweden. Thus in comparison, India's birth rate is more than twice as high or even more."* Further he notes, *"Not only birth rate is high, it has remained almost stable at a high level in very many years. In the 90 years or so since 1911, there has not been any marked decline. For example, it fell from 49 to 37 in 1971-1980 (and 18 till 1991), which amounts to very little considering the long time-span of nearly a century during which it has fallen."*

Steady growth in birth rate and low death rate is a very common feature of all under developed countries. There are various reasons – economic as well as non-economic – responsible for high birth rate in India.

As per the theory of demographic transition, India can be classified to be in her second stage of transition. The first phase was up to 1921, when both birth and death rates were high. After this stage, there was a low decrease in birth rate as well as death rate, resulting in population increase. After 1991, the death rate has gone down below 10. Now there is almost no possibility of this rate going still lower. This means we have reached the third stage of demographic transition as far as death rate is concerned. Birth rate can still go lower but it is almost impossible. This means, for many years to come population growth in India will continue at the present rate of growth.

The reasons for the high birth rate in India are varied. Poverty, religious and social attitudes, illiteracy, ignorance and non-availability of birth control devices and early marriageable age are some of the main reasons. Socio-economic development and birth rate are closely interrelated. Economic development has taken place in India but still it is not sufficient, while satisfactory social development still requires a considerable time span. In the lower strata of society children start working for the family at a very early stage, hence they prove to be asset to the family. On the other hand, survival rate of children among the poor people is very low due to unhealthy living conditions. In order to ensure their children's survival, they tend to have large number of children. Marriage in India is not just a social institution; it is a religious duty as well. The average marriageable age of females in India was 16 years. This meant a longer fertility period. This is also one of the reasons of high birth rate. Of course, the average marriageable age in 1981 is 18 years, but compared to the marriageable age in the developed countries, it is still very low. As suggested by V.G. Manker, the average marriageable age in the developed countries is 25 to 28 years. The importance of male child and lack of proper education in family planning are also vital social causes of high birth rate. When the society will obtain both social and economic development, then only there is a possibility of decrease in birth rate.

The situation regarding death rate is altogether different. In the beginning of the 20$^{th}$ century the death rate was as high as 43 per cent. Poverty, illiteracy, early marriage, infant mortality, lack of medial facilities, epidemics were the main reasons for high death rate. As Agarwal (1999) notes, death rate in India was 42.6 per thousand annual in 1901-10, it came to 31.2 during 1931-40 and was only 15 during 1971-80 and in 1986-91 and it was 10.8. This drastic fall in death rate is not only the result of economic development, but also control over epidemics, better health care facilities, green revolution in agriculture, nutritious food etc. are responsible for bringing down death rate in India after independence.

The density of population to day comes to 267 as against 216 in the year 1981. Thus, 51 more persons are occupying one square kilometer area than in 1981. In 1951 the number of persons per square kilometer was just 117. This means to day this number has almost doubled. The post independence India thus shows a remarkable growth in the density of population (Table - 3.3).

It is evident from the census of 1991 that the density of population in India varies from state to state from the maximum of 767 persons per square kilometer in West Bengal followed by Kerala (749), Bihar (497), U.P. (473), Tamilnadu (429) and Punjab (403) to the minimum of only ten persons per square kilometer in Arunachal Pradesh. Gujarat state stands below the average density of India with 211 persons per square kilometer.

Census results indicate that the density of population in India is gradually increasing. In 1901 the density was just 77 persons per square kilometer. It has increased to more than two and a half time than it was in 1901.

The adverse impacts of growing population density are evident especially in the urban areas. Delhi is one of the most populous cities of

India. Cities like Delhi face problems like over crowdedness, lack of hygiene in living areas as well as at work places, shortage of electricity, spread of epidemics, agglomeration of slums etc. The slums in turn breed crime and hostility. People living both in slums and the surrounding areas become victims of the hostility of population. The pollution problems of air, water, land and noise are very heavy in the highly populous cities like Delhi, Madras, Calcutta, Mumbai, etc. The next generation is forced to breathe in the atmosphere of acute degradation and lack of safety of life.

### 3.2 Sex Ratio

It is commonly observed that in the advanced countries of the world sex ratio rates in favour of females. But in India Kerala is the only state where sex ratio rates in favour of females. This indicates the importance given to the upbringing of female child, especially in matters of health and nutrition. In all other states of India the sex ratio rates in favour of males. Table - 3.4 indicates the proportion of females in rural as well as urban areas of India as per 1991 census.

It is evident from the figures given in the table - 3.4 that in rural and urban population sex ratio is imbalanced as there are only 894 females in urban areas, while in rural areas this ratio is 938 females per thousand males. In 1901 there were 970 females per thousand males, while in 1991 there were 927 females per one thousand males. This trend is found to be the same both in rural and urban areas. The decreasing rate of female population is a problem, which has alarmed the sociologists a great deal.

### 3.3 Urbanization

Urbanization is a process of transformation of population from rural sector to urban sector G.T. Trevertha (1969) defines urbanisation as "*a process of transformation of villages into towns and towns into cities.*" Further describing urbanization he states, "*The process involves the concentration of population in the urban areas. The level of urbanization can be defined as proportion of total population residing in urban areas.*" But it is not always considered proper to define an urban area with reference to population growth. According to Prof. Clarke (1972), "*Population growth is not necessarily a good index of population growth.*" Various criteria are used to define an urban area. It is a place where population is dense and majority of population is employed in various industrial sectors. Agriculture loses its importance in urbanisation. From administrative point of view, villages are run by panchayats, while cities are administered by either municipalities or corporations. The census of India collects and tabulates information on rural and urban areas separately and it is therefore an important source of data for the study of urbanisation. In 1991 reports, the census of India defines urban sector. According to this report, urbanisation must fulfill the following requirements. Firstly, all such places – urban areas – must have a municipality, corporation, cantonment board or notified town area committee. Secondly, such places must posses a minimum population of 5000. Thirdly, at least 75 per cent of male working population should be engaged in non-agricultural pursuits, and lastly, the density of population should be at least 400 persons per square kilometer.

Various economic factors are responsible for urbanisation. Due to centralization of industries, population also gets concentrated. Industrial centralization becomes more rapid and effective, simultaneously making labour force mobile. This process gets boosted because of better transportation and communication facilities. With the development of auxiliary industries in cities, employment opportunities are increased; hence, population migration towards cities becomes more rapid. This process is described as the 'Big Push'. Population migration is not just a 'Big Pull', i.e. attraction towards the glitter of the urban area. It is the result of better job opportunities, described as the 'Big Push'. It is the genuine cause of population migration. This attitude of population push towards cities becomes the pattern of life of the people; these changes are reflected in their life style. An individual starts spending for physical comforts. Education, upbringing of children, entertainment and better health facilities are some of the fields, which observe rapid progress with the process of urbanisation. On the other hand, the pressure of population on the urban areas creates an atmosphere of chaos in the fast developing countries like India. This chaos is due to socio-economic imbalance resulted from very rapid migration of population towards urban sectors. "*Urbanisation in fact, changes the whole attitude towards life and work*" (B.N. Ghosh).

It is not important when the process of urbanization started in any country as it happens parallel to economic development, but it is important to know how fast this process takes place. The rapidity of urbanisation can be observed from the contribution of industrial sector in the total national income. It is also important to study the impact and changes brought about in various fields because of the distribution of population resulting from urbanisation. One of the most important factors responsible for urbanization is migration of population from rural to urban area. Secondly, as time passes, there is natural growth of population in the urban sector, and thirdly, expansion of Government organization and trade and commerce are also responsible factors giving rise to urbanization. In a developing country like India, the first two causes of urbanization are more important.

Urbanization is a cyclic process. In the initial stage of the development of a country, it is observed to be slow, in the second stage, it becomes rapid, and then, in the last stage, it again becomes slow. The period of rapid growth of urbanization is quite long. In the world, the process of urbanization was very fast. This initial rapid growth continued for a long time as a result of new inventions in technology. Between the years 1800 and 1850 the rate of urbanization in the world was 4.3 per cent. This rate went upto nearly 9 per cent between 1850 and 1900. In 1960 the population of world in urban areas was 33 per cent. It has been estimated that by the end of the year 2000 the rate of urbanization will be nearly 55 per cent. This process of urbanization will go on increasing in the coming years. It has also been observed that the developing countries have greatly contributed in increasing the rate of population in the world (Table - 3.5). In the middle-income countries, the rate of urban populization is lower than the high-income countries, while in the lower income countries like India the rate of urban populization is around 25 per cent. But in these countries, the growth rate is higher than both high-income countries and middle-income countries. Compared to the urban population of the world this percentage is low, but the rate of population growth is high.

A very striking feature of India's urbanization is its large population. In 1991, India had an urban population of about 217 million (including Jammu and Kashmir and Assam). In 1981, India stood fourth in the world in urban population compared to China, the USA and the Republic of Russia. At present India is ranked second with high population in urban areas with regards to the rate of absolute population growth of the world. But compared to the total population this rate is only 25.72 per cent. In 1981-91, there was an increase of just 3.09 per cent in urban population in India, while before 1981 – according to census – the growth rate of urban population was higher than this. This reason for decline in the growth rate of urban population during this period was the acceleration of population growth in rural areas (Table - 3.6).

The rate of population growth in urban area depends on the factors stated below: (i) Growth due to population migration from rural to urban areas. (ii) Growth due to natural increase of urban population. (iii) Growth due to status change or settlement. (iv) Growth due to jurisdictional changes in boundaries of urban areas. The available data of changes in birth rate and death rate indicate the population growth in rural areas. Table - 3.7 indicates the average annual birthrate in India (per thousand population). As shown here (Table - 3.7) the natural increase rate is slightly higher in rural areas than in urban areas between 1971-80 and 1981-90. There has been an increase during 1981-90 as compared to 1971-80 in both rural and urban population. But this increase is more significant in case of rural population (1.4) than in case of urban population (0.3). This shows widening gap in the natural increase rate between rural and urban areas. During the period 1971-81 a decrease in migration from rural to urban area has been observed. The percentage of rural to urban migration of population was 41.40 per cent in 1951-61, it went low to 18.87 per cent in 1961-71, and in 1971-81 it was 18.40 per cent. Likewise, due to area re-classification also a decrease in urban population has been observed. In 1951-61, the growth rate – as a result of area classification – was 23.02 per cent, which went low to 18.33 per cent in 1961-71 and only slightly increased in 1971-81. As shown in table - 3.8, the rate of total population in the urban area has increased but it does not indicate increase in the growth rate of population.

Urbanization in India has not been a very rapid process. In 1901, one out of ten person lived in the city. In 1971 this rate was 1.5, in 1991 it was 1.4 and in 2001 this rate was 1.3. According to the report of 1991, the growth of population is rapid only in the cities already having large population. Excluding Jammu and Kashmir and Assam, 140 million out of 215 million of total populations living in urban area lived in 296 cities of India. In this category only those cities having the population of more than 1,00,000 are included. 69 per cent of the total urban population live in these cities is as large as 78.5 per cent. In the federation like India with her 25 states and 6 union territories, the highest urban population lives in the state of Maharashtra. According to 1991 census 3,05,42,000 people lived in the urban areas of Maharashtra, while the lowest urban population of 4,49,000 was in the state of Himachal Pradesh. The West Zone of India possessed the highest urban population, while East zone had the lowest urban population, which amounted to 16 per cent only. A disparate range of urban patterns is discernible in the geographic mosaic of India. Cities – particularly Metros – appear to be evenly dispersed. Strategies based on the primacy of single agglomerates, as in several smaller nations, are not applicable to India. Instead, a hierarchical pattern based on metros, cities and medium towns is available. Population growth has been observed in the cities having the population of more than one million. As per 1991 census Mumbai is ranked first with 12572 million of population, second is ranked Kolkata with 10916 million, Delhi and Madras are ranked third and fourth with the total population of 8375 million and 8361 million respectively.

### 3.4 Education

It can be observed from the experience of the developed countries that a rapid increase has been seen in production compared to increase in labour and physical capital. This is the result of increase in human capital. The development in human capital is a result of better health and educational facilities. Improved educational facilities have widened the horizons of human mind, and health facilities have improved health. Thus, human resource development has been achieved through mental and physical development of people. Human resource development is an important factor in economic development. It is very important because the society is made of various groups of individuals, which depend upon nature and quality of population. The quantitative aspect of population of a country depends upon the level of education of people. "*Education interacts and is inter-dependent with the process of economic development.*" Education is also influenced by social structure, policies and goals of development. On the other hand, education also influences economic and social development by inducing change in technology through the systematic application of scientific and other knowledge for specialized task to meet the challenges at different levels of developmental process of a country.

Education helps social development in two ways – it boosts human resource development and helps to increase human capital; i.e. productive population of a country. The expenditure on human development is also a kind of capital investment. "*(i) The cost of rearing and educating human beings is a real cost. (ii) The product of their labour adds to the national wealth. (iii) The expenditure on a human being that increases the product will ceteris peribus increase national wealth*" (B.K. Kiker, 1993).

Education is an indicator of human capital formation. This includes all levels of education – primary, secondary and higher education. Primary education is the foundation of all round educational progress and higher education is related to different high-level skills and science and technologies. This is the reason why it is important to know the proportion of population in different levels of education and also the number of people who give up their education and training in between. It is also necessary to know the number of people who are in high-level professions or occupations. These include, especially, the number of selected strategic occupation groups, scientist, engineers, managers, teachers of all levels, doctors, scientific and engineering technicians, nurses, medical assistants and persons who fall in the category of skilled workers.

It is necessary to find out the total proportion of education in India alongwith the proportion of education at different levels; i.e. the proportion of education in urban and rural sectors, in males and females, and the proportion of education in different age groups of the population to evaluate the contribution of education in socio-economic development of India.

It can be derived from the 1981 and 1991 census that the total rate of education in India has increased and the rate of both male and female education indicates an increase but side-by-side, the rate of illiteracy has also increased. According to census 2001 the total literacy rate of India is 65.38 per cent out of which male literacy rate is 75.88 per cent and female literacy rate is 54.16 per cent. The total increase in illiteracy is 18.35 per cent which includes 3.81 per cent increase in male illiteracy and 14.54 per cent increase in female illiteracy. The number of female literacy has touched 126.06 million, which shows 14.54 per cent of increase than that of in 1981 (Table - 3.9).

The table - 3.9 indicates increase in both male and female literacy as well as illiteracy but the study of female literacy is more important as an indicator of social awareness and development. The steps to increase female literacy are necessary as steps towards child health, nutritious food and also in creating awareness of family planning. The total number of illiterates in India (according to census 2001 report) is 29,62,08,952. The figure indicates the decrease in the total number of illiterates. The decadal decrease in illiterates is 3,19,58,336. Female literacy also helps to put check on fertility and control of IMR P.N. Haksar (1997) has recently commented, "*In all these years we should have diverted millions of rupees to education and culture... We then might have succeeded in making the demographic transition.*" Ashish Bose (1997) also agrees with Haksar on this issue. He has urged the Government "*to divert all available resources to provide 100 per cent literacy as soon as possible.*" Table - 3.10 indicates literates per thousand.

Table - 3.10 shows increase in male and female literacy rate. In pre-independence India, the rate of female literacy was very low. Of course, this has gradually increased in the post-independence era, but still it is low compared to the literacy rate in males. In Kerala the number of literate females was 862 per thousand in the year 1991, but the rate of female literacy was very low in the states of Rajasthan, Bihar and U.P.

One of the direct outcomes of the educational demographic transition is movement of population education structure from primary to secondary and secondary to higher education. The rate of formal education in both males and females in various age groups is taken as a criterion of social development. Accordingly, in primary education the individuals between the age of 5 and 14 are taken. The individuals between the age of 15 and 19 and between 20 and 24 are considered in secondary education and higher education respectively. This scheme can provide an indicator to find out the rate of education in primary, secondary and higher education as well as subsidiary education in India. This will also help to study the changes in age wise education pattern from 1981 to 1991 census results.

In India, primary education has not become universal even after fifty years of planning period. It is difficult to say whether it has been due to population growth or due to our wrong educational policy during the planning period. It is a well-known fact that higher education is far better in our country than many other countries. Table - 3.11 shows increase in higher education but still the number of women in higher education is very low. Even in overall educational pattern the number of females has been low compared to males. The rate of females in standards 1 to 5 was 28.1 per cent in 1950-51, which increased to 47.5 per cent in 1991-92. In higher education arts faculty recorded the highest 65.5 per cent of female students in 1991-92, while in engineering the rate of female students was recorded just 9.5 per cent. Compared to engineering, medical faculty recorded higher number of female students.

It is also necessary to final out the drop out ratio in all the sectors of education so that the reasons responsible for these drop outs can be arrived at. There are several socio-economic reasons as well as unavailability of necessary infrastructure for the high drop out ratio. One of the important social reasons is marriage at younger age – especially in rural communities. Secondly, children are still considered as an important source of income, hence they are forced to drop out at the time of economic crisis in the family.

The rate of drop out is very high even in higher education, which is evident from table - 3.12.

In the year 1994-95 Rs.312.8 per capita were spent for education in India, the total amount spent after education was just 3.5 per cent of the total expenditure of the country in that year. Compared to developed countries the rate of expenditure on education was very low. Generally the Governments in the developed countries do not spend very large amounts on education because most of the education, especially higher education, is a private affair. In the year 1990 the USA spent just 1.7 per cent on education. In UK and Germany the expenditure was 3.2 per cent and 0.6 respectively. But in India the scenario of education is totally different. Complete privatisation of education is not possible in India. Not only in India but in all developing countries the same situation prevails, hence the Governments have to play a vital role and spend a large amount of money for the promotion of education.

The United Nations has defined literacy as "*the ability of a person to read and write with understanding a short simple statement on his everyday life.*" According to this definition an individual who is at least ten years old and who can read and write and understand is considered literate. But in India the word literacy has been very loosely used. All those who can read and write simple sentences are considered as literate. In the developed countries like Japan and the USA no questions regarding primary education are included in samples collection for census information. But in the developing countries like India information regarding primary education has a very special importance.

Education is an important factor for the modernization of population because it has wide spread effects on an individual's life. Education plays a pivotal role as a determinant and decisive factor in marriageable age, fertility, mortality, population migration, quantity and quality of labour force, etc. Thus, education plays a manifold role in the socio-economic development of a country.

Marriage is an unavoidable and necessary institution in India. There has been a customary trend of child marriages, especially in the socially backward states of Rajasthan, Bihar and Uttar Pradesh. Though the Government has legalized the lowest marriageable age of 18 years for females and 21 years for males, more than 70 per cent marriages take place between the age of 13 and 18. If the rate of education increases, automatically the rate of child marriage – especially in women – will decrease. The period of the age groups of 13 to 18 is the period of obtaining secondary education but it has been noted that the rate of drop outs is very high among the individuals of this age group. The number of girl drop outs is very high. Fertility and education and religion and education are closely interrelated. As the rate of education is low, the rate of fertility is found to be higher. Education is very low in Muslim women compared to their Hindu counterparts. Because of low education and strong religious beliefs, the rate of fertility amongst Muslim women is high (Table - 3.13).

Education also affects greatly the rate of mortality. Naturally, educated population can take better care in bringing up their children and pay more attention to primary health. This helps a lot in bringing down mortality rate. Implementation of regular immunization programmes, awareness of preventive measures to keep serious diseases and epidemics at a bay, awareness of nutritive food and clean, hygienic habits come through education. These in turn help to bring down mortality rate. Due to education, geographic and occupational mobility of labour force increases resulting in the development of urban areas. As a result, rural sector gets transformed into towns. Thus education helps a great deal in bringing about all these demographic changes.

### 3.5 Infant Mortality Rate (IMR)

The Central Government of India announced its new population policy on 15 February 2002 in which socio-demographic goals to be achieved by the end of the decade were declared. One of the major targets of the new population policy is to bring down the rate of IMR, which will be 80 to 30 by the year 2010. In 1981 the IMR was 110 and reduced considerably in a decade but it is not adequate if the target is to bring it down still low. The

IMR in different time segments is shown in table - 3.14. As indicated in the table the IMR in the year 1997 was registered as 77.

In 1997, the IMR in the states of Orissa, Madhya Pradesh, Rajasthan and Utter Pradesh was recorded as 96, 94, 85 and 85 respectively, which does not draw a very happy picture of the coming years. In the states of Goa, Mizoram and Pondicherry the IMR was considerably low, but it was recorded the lowest of 12 in Kerala. In rural and urban sectors, also the IMR was different as indicated in table - 3.15.

The difference in IMR in rural and urban sectors was quite high in the year 1971 but gradually this difference has narrowed down. But still the difference in IMR in rural and urban sectors was 31 in 1997. It is also noteworthy that in the past few years the IMR has remained almost steady in the rural sector while in urban sector the decrease in IMR has been noted.

In the following discussion, an attempt has been made to examine the differences in IMR in various states of India in urban and rural sectors in the year 1997 as a sample. The IMR was recorded 11 and 15 in rural and urban sectors respectively in the state of Kerala, which was the lowest IMR in all the states of India. In rural Orissa the IMR was recorded as 100, being the highest IMR. In the urban sectors of Uttar Pradesh, the IMR was recorded 66, being the highest in urban sectors of all the states. Generally, it has been observed that the IMR in urban sectors was lower than in rural sectors but the state of Kerala was an exception where IMR was found higher in urban areas.

In Gujarat the IMR in rural areas was 69 while in cities it was 46, which comes to an average of 62, in both rural and urban sectors together. Even the urban areas in Rajasthan, Orissa, Uttar Pradesh and Madhya Pradesh were very backward in taking steps to increase health awareness. In these states, 80 per cent of women deliver their children at home with the help of untrained midwives in very unhygienic and dirty surroundings. This happens because of poverty and lack of education and awareness in women. The condition in these states might create an obstacle in bringing down the IMR by the target year 2010 as has been proposed in the new population policy.

Studies reveal that IMR and Child Mortality Rate (0-4 age group) are still high after all the efforts to bring them down. It is very high compared to the IMR of developed countries. Some of the causes for this situation are as follows: (i) People of all strata of society do not avail of the facilities provided by the Government. (ii) Women do not get enough advantage of the health programmes. (iii) Both TFR and mortality rates are still very high. (iv) Women are forced into pregnancy against their wish because of the importance of male child in the family. Thirteen million women in India get married below 18 years. The number of women entering into motherhood below 20 years was 2.2 million in 1961. This member increased to 3.3 in 1988. The percentage of pregnancy in elderly women has also increased. The rate of pregnancy in elderly women was 13 per cent in 1971, which increased to 23 per cent in 1988. In many states of India, because of the lack of public awareness, this condition still prevails.

It is noted that the IMR in females is low but mortality rate in females under four years is high. The reason for this is obvious – female child is not taken proper care of by her parents (Table - 3.16).

Expectation of life at birth by sex in India and major states is shown in table - 3.17. This indicates the fact that improvement in expectation of life at birth for females has been faster than expectation of life at birth for males in India. In the beginning of mortality transition females were relegated to a disadvantageous position that led to larger decline in the overall sex ratio in the 1960s. In 1961 female-male sex ratio was 941 and it declined to 930 in 1971. In fact, mortality differentials reached their peak in the 1960s and had begun to decline in 1970s. In 1991, the female ratio was 927. After this, there has not been a rapid decrease in this ratio. There has been an average increase in longevity. Though women are not given enough importance in society, the death rate in elderly women has considerably decreased, but death rate in female children is still very high. People have become aware of health care. The combined efforts of the government and people play an important role in improving the health awareness, yet these efforts are insufficient. In 1994-95 the amount spent after health was just Rs. 133.5 per capita.

The infant mortality rate is considered to be a sensitive indicator not only of the health status of population but also of the level of human development in the context of education, economic condition, nutrition etc. In India in the recent times there has been an acceleration in the pace of decline in the IMR after a period of stagnation.

IMR declined at 3.6 per cent per year during 1987-92 compared to 2.2 per cent during the earlier time period. This acceleration in the speed of decline in IMR was noticed in most states during 1987-92. It was quite high at more than 5 per cent per year in the states of Bihar (5.8 per cent), Gujarat (6.7 per cent), Kerala (9.3 per cent), Tamilnadu (5.2 per cent) and Utter Pradesh (5.0 per cent), and quite low – at less than 2 per cent per year – in the states of Karnataka (0.5 per cent), Madhya Pradesh (1.8 per cent), Orissa (1.3 per cent) and West Bengal (1.4 per cent).

## 3.6 Gujarat

### Structure and Growth of Population in Gujarat

Gujarat is one of the high income states of India. The other three are Punjab, Maharashtra and Haryana. A state whose per capita net domestic produce is Rs.7500 and above in 1993-94 has been considered a high-income state (P.V. Rajeev, 1999). Industries, agriculture and fishery are the actual asset of a state that determines the level of its economic growth and prosperity. The main focus of this discussion is to provide understanding and an overview of growth, distribution and socio-economic structure of population. The discussion will also help in understanding the causes of regional development of all districts in Gujarat.

Gujarat has a total area of 196024 square kilometers. It is also one of the highly populated states of India with a total estimated population of 5.06 crores as per census 2001. It is also one of the socio-economically advanced states of India. Here urbanization is very high. The state has the second highest urban population. First comes Maharashtra with 38.69 per cent urban population, while the urban population in Gujarat is 34.49. The rate of urban population in the whole of India is recorded 25.72 in the year 1991.

The population growth rate of Gujarat during the period between 1981-91 was 21.19 per cent, which has gone up to 22.66 in the period 1991-2000 (Table - 3.18). This indicates that the growth rate of Gujarat is near about the growth rate of the nation, which was 22.71 per cent during 1981-91. Since 1901, the population of the state has gone up from a mere 91 lakh to 506 lakh, which is five times more. During 1981-91 the total population of Gujarat was 413 lakh. The first two decades of this century witnessed the period of population decline, but then it followed the steady growth of population during 1921-1951. The population growth accelerated with a high growth rate during the post independence period. Table - 3.18 shows trend of population growth in Gujarat from 1901 to 2001.

The population growth in Gujarat follows the similar pattern of population growth in India (table - 3.18). The average population growth was

5.40 per cent till 1921. After that the growth became more rapid, but after 1951 a remarkably rapid population growth is seen in Gujarat. The figures of the last census indicate that the decadal growth pattern of population during the last decade of the $20^{th}$ century. As per census 2001 the population of Gujarat has touched the figure of 506 lakh.

According to the figures available from 1991 census records Ahmedabad was the most populated district with its total population of 48,02,000 and the Dangs was the least populated district with 1,44,000. Second stood Kheda with 34,41,000, while Surat was third with its total population of 33,98,000. In Gandhinagar district the total population in 1991 was 4,09,000, but being the capital city of Gujarat and the centre of all political and administrative activities, its socio-economic development is expected to be rapid, which is clearly observed in the last decade.

The state is divided into five geographic regions – Saurashtra, North Gujarat, Kutch, Central Gujarat and South Gujarat. Among these regions North Gujarat is ahead of all in population growth, while South Gujarat region possesses maximum total population. Gujarat stands second in India in population growth with 36.29 per cent.

### 3.7 Density of Population in Gujarat

The density of population in Gujarat comes to 211 in 1991 as against 174 in 1981. Thus, 37 more persons occupy per square kilometer area than in

1981. It has increased to more than four times compared to 1901. In 1901, this number was just 50 persons per square kilometer. In the post-independence Gujarat there has been a remarkable growth in the density of population. In 1953 the density of population was 83. When Gujarat separated from the united state of Bombay and emerged as an individual state in 1961 the density of population was 105. According to census records the population density of India in 1991 was 274 it while in Gujarat it was 211 per square kilometer.

It is evident from the Census 1991 that the density of population varies from district to district level from the maximum of 630 persons per square kilometer in Gandhinagar followed by Ahmedabad (551) and Kheda (478) to minimum of only 28 persons per square kilometer in the Kutch district. Surat district stands fourth with 444 persons per square kilometer. In Gandhinagar district the city Gandhinagar covers a very large area and yet the population of Gandhinagar is much more than the land area covered by the city. Kutch is the least populated area because major part of the land area is a desert. But the distribution of population is an ever-changing phenomenon. So many socio-economic-geographic factors are responsible for the ever-changing population patterns. "*The distribution patterns of population density would surely be changed in time to come because this distribution is only a stage, not even a stable one, is an evolution whose progress we cannot at present altogether understand*" (Blache, 1952). The density of population in various districts of Gujarat is mainly in the urban areas. It is evident from the fact that more than 40 per cent of population lives in urban areas. The Dangs possesses less population but the number of women is more compared to other districts, while in Surat district the number of women is less.

### 3.8 Urbanization

Urbanization is an important phenomenon of population redistribution. It is a continuous process – attached with socio-economic development. S.D. Maurya (1958) considers urban areas as nodes of settlements and the real 'foci' of social contacts and economic growth. He states, "*They do not exist for themselves alone, rather they are part of a complex whole and serve the surrounding countryside with which they are spatially and functionally knit together.*" In respect of urbanization Gujarat ranks fourth amongst the states of India with proportion of urban population at 34.49 per cent as compared to 25.7 per cent for the rest of the country. As per Primary Census Report of 2001 the percentage of urban population has touched 37.67 and by the year 2011 it is likely to reach at 42.42 per cent. It is evident from the census 2001 Primary Report that more than 76 per cent of urban population of the state resides in the class-I cities, while it was only 19.59 per cent in 1901 and only 36.07 per cent in 1951 (Table - 3.19).

The process of urbanization has been very fast in Gujarat since its formation. It is evident from table 3.19 that in 1961 about 25.76 per cent of total population of the state was residing in urban places. This percentage is continuously rising. The urban ratio of population was recorded 34.49 per cent in 1991. In the same year this figure was 25.13 per cent for India. In 1991 the total population of Gujarat was distributed 2.71 crore and 1.42 crore respectively in rural and urban areas. Thus, there has been an increase in the percentage of urban population in the state from 31.10 to 34.49 per cent since 1981. As shown in the table - 3.19, in 1991 every 65 persons out of 100 still lived in rural areas in Gujarat state. As per the 1991 records Ahmedabad district possessed 74.89 percent of urban population, which is the highest in the state. Second stood Surat with 50.56 per cent. There are many districts, which contributed to urban population between 40 per cent and 50 per cent. These districts are Jamnagar, Rajkot, Gandhinagar and Vadodara. Banaskantha, Sabarkantha, Panchmahals and Dangs districts have less than 11 per cent of urban population. Banaskantha has the lowest to 10.19 per cent in the year 1991.

Considering each urban agglomeration as one unit the total number of urban units recorded in 1991 were 264. The distribution of urban centres at district level is also not equal. The number of urban centres in Ahmedabad district comes to 25, which is the highest, while in the Dangs and Gandhinagar districts the number of urban centres is 2 and 3 respectively. Taking into consideration the total urban population in the state the Dangs possesses minimum urban population, while in Gandhinagar it is as high as

40 per cent. This indicates that in Gandhinagar district only the city Gandhinagar possesses the highest urban population.

Table - 3.20 indicates the number of urban population in the cities of Gujarat recorded in 1991 census. Ahmedabad city possesses highest number of population, while Surat is ranked second. Gandhinagar shows very rapid progress while Porbandar indicates the lowest rate of population growth. Ahmedabad is ranked first in the density of population while in Surat it is proportionately low because of geographical expansion of the city. The density of population in Morbi city is the lowest. The number of female population per ten thousand males is low in Surat compared to the other cities of Gujarat. The reason for this is clear. There is a constant flow of population in Surat from the various states of India due to rapid industrialization of the city and its surrounding areas.

### 3.9 Sex Ratio

It has been generally observed that in the advanced countries of the world sex ratio rules in favour of females. In India Kerala is the only state where sex ratio rules in favour of females, which indicates the importance given to the upbringing of female child, especially in matterns of health and nutrition. In all other states of India the sex ratio rules in favour of males. Table - 3.21 (A and B) shows the proportion of females in rural as well as in urban areas of Gujarat as per 1991 census.

There are 213.56 lakh males and 199.54 lakh females in the state comprising 51.70 per cent and 48.30 per cent of total population respectively. Thus sex ratio comes to be 934 females per thousand of male population as against 932 in the year 1981. It is higher than the average sex ratio of India (927). However, in rural and urban population sex ratio is imbalanced as there are only 907 females per thousand males in urban areas, while in rural areas this rate is 950 females per thousand males. It is also noteworthy that the sex ratio in the state has, from census to census, been always above the national average since 1961.

The ratio of male and female population in different districts of Gujarat varies considerably. In the Dangs district, this ratio is the highest with 983 females per thousand males. It is followed by Amreli with 982 females, while in Ahmedabad district it is the lowest with 899 females per 1000 males. This indicates that in the districts where urban population is higher, the number of female population is low. In the cities where the density of population is more, the ratio of women is relatively low, while in the cities with low population density the number of women is relatively high. This depends upon the economic activities of the area. In the large cities where industries flourish population from other states migrates in search of employment. In such places, due to migration, the number of female population is comparatively lower. However, places where economic activities depend upon agriculture, the number of female population is relatively high compared to the sex ratio by the other cities of Gujarat. The number of women is relatively low in Surat for the prime reason likely to be that for the last few decades Surat is rapidly developing as an industrial area. Not only in Surat, but also in all the major cities of Gujarat the migration of male population is a common phenomenon, "*It appears basically due to males migrating out in large number in the search of employment. The sex differentials in any area are determined by sex ratio (i) at birth, (ii) the differential mortality rates of the two sexes and (iii) sex selectivity in migration*" (L. Singh and D. Nath – 1981).

### 3.10 Health

The health infrastructure has been able to achieve a significant improvement in the health status of the people of the state. The gap between a state's birth and death rates are the two variables determining a states population growth. Differential movements in the two rates can provide an explanation of the pattern of population growth. The birth and death rates in urban and rural areas are different as the factors affecting these rates are varied, hence the changes brought about in the pattern of population due to changes in death and birth rates are also different. Infant Mortality Rate is also one of the principal indicators of health. Decline in IMR indicates better health in the region. Table - 3.22 indicates these changes in the state between 1961 and 1996.

Birth rate and death rate in Gujarat in 1996 were 25.7 and 6.2 respectively. In urban areas birth rate was 23.0 and in rural areas it was 26.9. Even to day birth rate is higher in rural areas compared to the urban areas. Death rate is also higher in the rural areas. The total birth rate in 1961 was 45.7 which decreased to 28.1 in 1991. But decrease in death rate has been a slow process compared to the decrease in birth rate in the state.

The factors responsible for high birth rate are economic, social and religious. Apart from these three main factors, there are some other factors responsible for high birth rate. These are: (i) Children are considered a major source of income, especially in the economically backward society. According to cost benefit analysis theory the income raised by children is more than the expenses parents have to put up in bringing them up. (2) Marriageable age in both males and females is low. (3) According to social customs and religious beliefs it is important to have male child in the family. All these are important factors for high birth rate.

Decrease in IMR is an important indicator of social development. It also indicates many other changes taking place in the social structure of the society. Increase in female education, increase expenditure and proper care on the upbringing of children, availability of nutritious food for expectant mothers and children, implementation of health care and immunization programmes – all these are responsible factors in bringing down IMR and increasing longevity. Between 1991 and 1996 the life expectancy in males was 60.94 while in women it was 62.74. This ratio was higher than the longevity ratio is India. IMR in Gujarat is also comparatively lower than the IMR in India. The reasons for this change are clearly evident. In the last few years Primary Health Care Centres have been opened in rural and also in very interior tribal areas of the state. There is at least one Primary Health Care Center per one lakh of population. Government as well as Non-Government Organizations are active in the field of health care. Family Welfare Centres organize health awareness programmes for the people. Gujarta is one of the four states of India connected with WHO. The number of Primary Health Centres and sub centres functioning in the urban and rural sectors of the state has increased to 960 and 7274 respectively at the end of the year 1997-98 from 251 and 2120 respectively in 1980-81. With regard to medical institutions the state has 26 General Hospitals, 23 Colleges and 21 taluka level hospitals. The diseases like Maleria has been brought under control. The Government for health spends average of Rs.143 per head. In the eighth five-year plan Rs.17,606 lakh were spent for various health programmes in the state (Socio-Economic Review, Gujarat State, 1999-2000).

### 3.11 Literacy

Gujarat state being economically advanced compared to other states and largely urbanized, is also educationally very advanced compared to many other states of India. There are some basic differences between a literate and an educated person. One who can read and write with understanding in at least one language is considered as literate, while an educated person must have acquired some schooling. Literacy or education is not merely functional, but it also has very close linkage with various aspects of social groups. Above all, it increases the receptivity of social group of the stimuli of socio-economic and politico-cultural developments. It strengthens the capacity of the society to respond to it and thereby promote the process of development.

In 1991 the total literacy in the state was 61.29 per cent. Thus the state, however, achieved an increase of 11.39 per cent in literacy over 1981 when it was 49.90 per cent. It should be noted that there is a remarkable increase in literacy in females. Table - 3.23 indicates that the rate of education in India has increased by 8.95 while in Gujarat the increase in literacy is 11.39 per cent. In 1991 Gujarat stood $9^{th}$ in literacy amongst all the states of India.

As table - 3.24 indicates, literacy is not uniform in all the districts of the state but varies considerably from the highest of 87.11 per cent in Gandhinagar district to the lowest of only 39.29 per cent in Banaskantha district..

As table - 3.25 figures reveal, that literacy is higher in urban places than in the rural areas. Gandhinagar district followed by Vadodara with 80.88 per cent, Valsad with 78.94 per cent, while the lowest literacy – 68.12 per cent – is in the Banaskantha district achieved highest urban literacy of 87.82 per cent (Not shown in the table - 3.25). In case of rural areas, districts of

Banaskantha with 35.94 per cent, Panchmahals with 39.89 per cent, the Dangs with 43.41 per cent and Kutch district with 44.95 per cent cover the bottom line. The districts of Gandhinagar with 86.62 per cent, Mehsana with 61.86 per cent, Kheda with 62.10 per cent are on the top.

In general, the literacy among females is lower than in males. Highest literacy in male population is recorded 93.21 per cent in Gandhinagar district, while the lowest 58.89 is found in Banaskantha. Likewise, highest literacy rate in female population is found in Gandhinagar (80.51 per cent) and Ahmedabad (62.39 per cent). Banaskantha with 22.50 per cent and Panchmahals with 27.31 per cent are poor in female literacy. It is also observed that more urban people – both males and females – are literate compared to rural population of this state because of more and better educational facilities available in the urban centres. It is remarkably true that female literacy is picking up faster than male literacy, which in turn is bound to have a voluntary effect on the pace of literacy in general.

In 1995-96 the number of institutions for primary education in the state were 33119 which increased to 33822 in the year 1996-97, and the total number of pupils was 73.04 lakh and 73.41 lakh respectively in the year 1995-96 and 1996-97. The state Government has introduced District Primary Education Programme (DPEP) for the spread of education in the state with the monetary help from the World Bank. The World Bank has contributed 40 crore rupees which comes to 85 per cent of the total expenses of the programme. The remaining 15 per cent is borne by the State Government. Initially Banaskantha, Panchmahals and the Dangs districts have been selected for the implementation of this programme. In the ninth five-year plan period, all the districts of Gujarat are covered under DPEP.

There were 5713 institutions for secondary education and higher education in the year 1995-96 and the number of students availing of this facility was 19.25 lakh, while in 1996-97 there were 5767 institutions for higher studies and the number of students was 19.24 lakh. There were 8 universities and 436 colleges in 1996-97. The ratio of pupil-teacher in primary education in 1993-94 was 1 teacher per 45 pupils in Gujarat, while in India it was 1.50. In secondary education the student teacher ratio in Gujarat was 1 teacher per 26 students, while in India it was 1.30. In higher education this ratio was 1.31 in Gujart and 1.34 in India. The average per capita expenditure on education was Rs. 3,494 in 1991 in Gujarat.

### 3.12 Occupational Structure

In developing human resources the active agents of modernization are the human beings. They are capable of building a strong economic base. For socio-economic development strong, active human beings and more capital are required. "*They alone can accumulate capital, exploit natural resources and build political and social organizations*" (The Gazette of India, Vol. III, 1977). It is obvious that the total population is divided into two groups: active and non-active. The total population of a state is not so important for its level of economic development as the active group, which is generally employed in various occupations.

Generally, the total population is mainly divided into (i) main workers, (ii) managerial workers and (iii) non-workers, in terms of economics. The main workers are known as working population. According to 1991 census there are 14 lakh main workers, 25 lakh managerial workers and 247 lakh non-workers in Gujarat. Thus the main workers constitute about 34.12 per cent of the total population of the state. The total active population includes 16620 ('000) persons and non-active population includes 24690 ('000) persons.

In the total population of the state – 16620 ('000) there are 12305 ('000) males and 4315 ('000) females engaged in various economic activities. They form the labour force of the state. Thus, 40.23 per cent of the total population of the state is comprised of main workers as against 37.46 per cent for India. The total labour force include 34.12 per cent main workers, out of which 13.73 per cent are females. In 6.11 per cent total managerial workers there are 12.23 per cent females. Thus there are 25.96 per cent females in the total work force in Gujarat.

Table - 3.26 shows the proportion of male and female workers engaged in primary, secondary and tertiary sectors in Gujarat and all India. As shown here, the percentage of main workers engaged in the primary sector is lower than the percentage of main workers at all India level, but the number of women workers engaged in agriculture is higher than that of India, while in secondary and tertiary sectors the number of main workers in Gujarat is higher than that of India. The Dangs district has the highest percentage (44.88) of main workers as well as the highest percentage (40.34) of female workers in Gujarat. In Surat, Valsad and Bharuch districts the percentage of main workers is very high. This comes to 39.4, 38.47 and 37.20 per cent respectively. This means the South Gujarat region has higher number of main workers. The lowest percentage (29.82) of main workers is found in Gandhinagar district and amongst them, the lowest percentage (8.86) of female workers is also seen in Gandhinagar district.

Population of Gujarat state indicates rapid growth but the sex ratio has been decreasing since the beginning of the 20$^{th}$ century. The state is agro-urban in character. Most of its population lives in rural areas. Urbanization in Gujarat is in its economical transition stage and is quite high in comparison to the nation. Literacy has increased considerably during the planning period. Urban areas are educationally advanced in comparison to rural areas. However, it is noted that females have lower literacy rate than males, both in rural and urban areas. In the state most females are economically non-active, hence their participation in labour force is very small, but it is higher than that of India. The state is predominantly agricultural and the majority of its population depends on agriculture for the livelihood. It is observed that female workers are mostly engaged in agricultural activities. The occupational distribution pattern of the state reveals the true character of a developing agro-industrial society.

### 3.13 Surat

The present study focuses on Surat for micro analysis. It is, therefore, essential to briefly discuss demographic features of the city.

Surat is India's $12^{th}$ and Gujarat's $2^{nd}$ most populous city. Located in South Gujarat, it became the $11^{th}$ metropolis in 1991, as it crossed 1 million population mark (Census 1991). The current estimated population of Surat is 24,33787 (Census 2001, Provisional Population Tables). It has experienced a very rapid population growth in the last two decades, and now the city possesses the largest population in Gujarat, after Ahmedabad. During the last four census decades; i.e. 1961-71, 1971-81, 1981-91 and 1991-2001 Surat registered the highest population growth. The current population growth rate of the city is 62.38 per cent (Census 2001 Provisional Data).

### 3.14 Historical and Religious Significance

A small trading centre of the $15^{th}$ and $16^{th}$ centuries, Surat has transformed into a fast-expanding metropolis. It is a complex process spread over several hundred years through changes in economic profile, administrative structure, physical boundaries and demographic composition.

The present day Surat has a glorious historical background dating back to 300 B.C. Originally a small Hindu town Suryapur, it has undergone significant changes over the years. In the past, it had gained status as one of the most important oceanic port and commercial centre of the Western India during 16th and 17th centuries. During 10th and 13th centuries it was ruled by Hindu rulers. "*In 1407 it was incorporated with the Muslim Sultanate of Gujarat to which it belonged until it was taken it by Akbar the Great in 1573 in the course of his campaign for the conquest of the province of Gujarat*" (The Gazette of India, Vol. III, 1977). During Akbar's regime the city became a prominent trade centre and a flourishing port. The Mughal period saw both the expansion of the city and of population. It became a moderately large, well-built place. From here the annual pilgrimage of Mecca embarked, giving the city a religious importance. "*Surat at the turn of the 177th century from all contemporary evidence had achieved a prosperity it had never known before*" (B.G. Gokhale, 1979).

In the early 17th century, the British began their trade with Surat. In 1757 when the British took over the administrative charge of the city. Other European merchants from Portugal, France and Netherlands had already established their trading relations with Surat. With the entry of the European traders the decline of the Mughals started. During the early British regime Surat further expanded in area and population, and in the beginning of the 20th century it was well connected by rail, roads and bridges with all the important places in the country.

Apart from the European merchants, the Arabs, Turks, Jews and Iranian traders also had settled in Surat and they expanded their trading activities with the neighbouring countries like Malaya, Burma, Jawa, Sumatra, Sri Lanka and the countries of the Persian Gulf and also with the important cities in India like Ahmedabad, Delhi, Agra, Burhanpur etc.

Surat was not only famous for its trading activities, but also for its manufacturing activities. The East India Company got its ships built and repaired from the Surat dockyard. Even the Dutch and the French also got their war ships built in Surat. The ship building activities engaged nearly 7000 to 8000 workers (Government of Gujarat, 1991). With the rise of the port of Bombay, the decline of Surat as a port and centre of trade took place. The decline of Surat as a centre of trade and commerce was rather abrupt. Various geographical, economic and political factors were responsible for this decline. In the early 19$^{th}$ century other industries like cotton textile and Zari and Kinkhab manufacturing units provided employment to the majority of population. However, except cotton textile industry, the Zari and Kinkhab units were small scale, usually managed at household level. After independence the evolution of population and handloom industrial units provided scope for commercial activities. Art silk and several other auxiliary industries were also established in Surat. These included engineering units producing machinery for art silk and Zari industries. Diamond cutting, polishing and processing units also dragged people from various parts of the state in large number to Surat. The majority of the diamond processing units are in the small sector.

The last two decades of the $20^{th}$ century witnessed vast and rapid industrial and mercantile changes of Surat and its surrounding areas. Many big industrial houses were attracted by the developmental potentials of Surat. In the Hazira belt known as the industrial belt, large scale industries have come up. Reliance, Larsen and Toubro, NTPC, KRIBHCO, ESSAR, ONGC, Gujarat Gas Company have come up and they are "*involving total investment of nearly Rs.27,000 crores*" (Ashim Dasgupta, 1978). In the Southern part of the city there are medium and small industrial units of GIDC. The sugar, yarn and textile industries are located in the Northern part of the city.

### 3.15 Demographic Profile of the City

Surat was a walled city. But in the past few years it has remarkably expanded both geographically and demographically. The city has also gone through all round progress. The rate of migrated people from other parts of Gujarat and outside Gujarat is more than 65 per cent. Four lakh people in Surat are migrated from Saurashtra, while from Uttar Pradesh and Bihar almost eight lakh people have come to Surat is search of employment. In 1966 Surat came to the status of corporation and in each census period its geographic area has expanded. Because of this parallel expansion of the geographical boundaries and population migration, it has become easy to find out the net increase of population in Surat. The area of the city has expanded five times from 8.18 square kilometer in 1901 to 112.28 square kilometer in 2001. Table - 3.27 indicates the population growth with the area expansion of Surat. The city has experienced the fastest growth at the rate of 62.68 per cent during 1991-2001. If the entire urban area of Surat is taken into account, the total population growth rate is as high as 85 per cent.

Surat is divided into six zones for the administrative purposes. It is also sub divided into 34 wards for the purpose of the formulation of the corporation (election purposes). These six zones are, (i) the Central Zone (inner city), (ii) the Eastern Zone (Varachha area), (iii) the Northern Zone (Katargam and Ved Road), (iv) the Western Zone (Rander and Adajan), (v) the Southern Zone (Udhana and Pandesara) and (vi) the South West Zone (Athwalines, Bhatar and Ghoddod Road).

According to the Provision Report of 2001 census 406018 people live in the slums, which comes to 16.68 per cent of the total population of Surat. There are 241524 males and 164494 females living in the slums.

### 3.16 Total Population and Density of Population

Six cities of Gujarat have the status of corporation. Surat stands second in total population next to Ahmedabad, and first in population density (Table - 3.28). The density of population has increased by 33 per cent during 1999-2001, but the geographical area of the city has not expanded during the last decade. Upto 1991 the population density was not recorded to be very high (Table - 3.29).

The estimated population in the Central Zone in 2001 is 706012, which comes to 30 per cent of the total population of the city. The density of population is the highest in Central Zone (Table - 3.30).

Surat city is divided into two parts, the old city and the new city. In the old city population has constantly increased but the density has marked a marginal decline in the last decade resulting in a corresponding increase in the density of population in the inner periphery. But now there is almost no scope for population increase in the old city. As the prices of land in the inner city are rising unexceptionally and almost no unused land is left in the city, people have started shifting to far away areas. This is the reason why areas like Rander, Adajan, Piplod, Bhatar are experiencing burden of population. The reasons are, land is comparatively cheaper, transport facilities are better and the newly built bridges on the river Tapi has made transportation of people and goods faster and more convenient. Moreover, these are safer residential areas.

### 3.17 Health

The average birth rate and death rate of the city during 1991-2001 was 23.70 per cent and 4.65 per cent respectively, and the Infant Mortality Rate during this period was 21.51 per cent. In the 1980s, the birth rate was 28.60

per cent, death rate was 6.69 per cent and IMR was 30.93 (A. Ghosh and S. Sami Ahmed, 1996). Both the death rate and IMR of Surat are lower than those of the other urban areas of Gujarat. The IMR in the year 1971 was 68 which reduced to 20.82 in the year 2000.

The figures indicate rapid decline in the IMR. The credit for the decline in death rate and IMR goes to the Heath Department of the Surat Municipal Corporation. The Corporation has under taken various schemes for child development like "Anganwadi" (children's play centres) and total immunization projects in collaboration with and help from WHO (1978). Various Non-Government Organizations and Women/Social Organizations have also contributed a fair share in carrying out these programmes successfully. The Surat Municipal Corporation has already surpassed its targets in the immunization programmes undertaken by the Corporation during 1991-2000. These immunization programmes include vaccination for B.C.G., Polio, D.P.T., Measles, D.T., T.T. etc. as indicated in table - 3.32.

### 3.18 Sex Ratio

According to 2001 census the sex ratio of Surat district is 835, which is the lowest in all districts of Gujarat. The sex ratio in Choryasi taluka is 722 while in Surat urban area it is 760 and in Surat city it is 774. Obviously the ratio of female population is lower in Surat compared to other cities because of the peculiar economic and industrial infrastructure of the city.

As table - 3.33 indicate, there were 839 females per thousand males in Surat in the year 1991. The ratio of female population is constantly declining in Surat but in the last decade; i.e. 1991-2001 it has recorded to be the lowest. At the same time Surat has undergone the highest industrial development. The labour force coming to Surat obviously consists of males, and they generally prefer to come as single earners leaving their families behind. This is the obvious reason why the female ratio is low in Surat. Secondly, the families migrated from other states to Surat happen to belong to male dominated societies, hence they do not prefer girl child in the family. The ratio of females in the slums of Surat is 681 per hundred males, which is very low compared to the other areas of Surat city.

### 3.19 Literacy

In 2001 the overall literacy of Surat is 83.35 which was 75.97 in 1991. The literacy rate has gone up in the last decade. Of course, the contribution of female population in bringing up the literacy rate in Surat cannot be ignored. According to the 1991 census the rate of literate women in Surat was 68.09 per cent which has increased to 76.73 per cent in 2001, while literacy rate in males has increased by one per cent. There were 83.41 per cent literate males as against 82.52 per cent in 1991 (Table - 3.34). Large-scale variations in the ward wise literacy rate are found in Surat. The lowest literacy rate is in Nana Varachha which is 47.74 per cent out of which the literacy rate in females is just 27.66 per cent, while ward no. 14 - Rander - possesses the highest literacy rate which comes to 96.26 per cent. The literacy rate in the slums is 67.46 per cent out of which male literacy rate is 75.43 per cent and female literacy rate is 55.14 per cent.

The overall literacy rate in Surat city has grown during the last three decades from 58 per cent in 1971, the rate has increased to 88.41 per cent. Among females, the literacy rate has, however, been consistently low about 47 per cent in 1971,51 per cent in 1981, 68.05 per cent in 1991 and 76.73 per cent in 2001, compared to male literacy rate of 66 per cent, 68 per cent, 82.49 per cent and 88.49 per cent respectively for the corresponding years.

### 3.20 Occupational Distribution of Population

Surat is the centre of all trading activities and industries in the South Gujarat region. The growing population of the city is responsible for the metro status of the city. There are nearly four lakh people in Surat from the out skirts of the city. These people are classed as floating population. Apart from the floating population, stable population is also increasing. This increase can be attributed to the migration of workers from different parts of Gujarat as well as from other states of India like Maharashtra, Orissa, Uttar Pradesh, Bihar, Rajasthan, etc. They are known as Khandesis, Malis, Bhaiyas and Marwaris respectively. Migrants from Saurashtra are mostly engaged in the diamond processing units while Malis and Khandesis are engaged in the textile manufacturing units of the city. Migrants from Uttar Pradesh, Rajasthan, Haryana, Punjab and from other parts of Gujarat are engaged in sales, production, processing, repairs and services under the self-employment category. Table - 3.35 shows occupational distribution of the population of Surat.

The central part of the city is known as the old city. This area and its peripheries are mostly occupied by upper and middle class people. The study of the population residing in the old city can be conducted religionwise as well as caste-wise. Hindus and Jains mostly reside in Gopipura, Nanavat, Sagrampura and Ambaji Road areas of the old city, while Patels are concentrated in Mahidharpura, Khatris in Salabatpura, Ghanchi-Gola-Ranas in Zampa Bazar area. Among the Muslims, Bohras are concentrated in Zampa Bazar and Memons in Muglisara and Bhagatalow, Parsis are pocketed in Nanpura and Shahpore areas. Machhis, Kharvas and the low-income-group Muslims live in Badekhan Chakla, Kadar Shah Ni Nal, Navsari Bazar and Saiyedpura areas of the old city.

The peripheral areas of Ashwanikumar Road, Katargam, Varachha, Ved, Dabholi, Bhestan, Pandesara and Udhana have fast developed as industrial areas. The labour force residing in these areas do not belong to any particular district or state, yet from the proportion of population belonging to particular places it can be classified as under: People from Saurashtra live in Ved, Varachha and Katargam areas while migrants from Maharashtra are generally found in Udhana, Pandesara, Bamroli and Limbayat areas. Upper class Marwaris and Punjabis prefer Bhatar Road, Athwa Lines and Ghoddod areas to live in. All those who are economically sound prefer these posh areas and even Surtis who belong to upper class have shifted to these areas. Both the original Surtis and migrants work hand in hand in business and industries. The contribution of migrants in industries and professions, both as manufacturers and labourers, is considerably large. In 1991 the total population of Surat was 14,98,817 out of which there were 9,86,491 non-workers and 5,12,326 were workers.

As indicated in table - 3.36, 55.35 per cent of total workers were engaged in manufacturing, processing and in other household industries, while 18.70 per cent were occupied in trade and commerce, and 13.20 per cent were engaged in other services. This shows that more than 50 per cent of the total population of Surat was engaged in industries and manufacturing units, both big and small. The rate of marginal workers was very small, just 0.67 per cent.

### 3.21 Family Planning

Birth rate and death rate are constantly decreasing as a result of successful efforts of both the Health Department of the Surat Municipal Corporation and National Family Welfare Programme. It is remarkable that the Health Department of the SMC has successfully surpassed the goals set by the Government of India under National Immunization Programmes. Simultaneously, the Family Welfare Centres of SMC have also succeeded in their family planning goals. According to the reports submitted by all the 32 Primary Health Centres (on 1-4-2002) run by the SMC there were 2,39,768 eligible couples for family planning in the year 2002. Out of these eligible couples, 85.06 per cent have adopted various family planning methods as indicated in table - 3.37, 91.52 per cent of the married women in the age group of 25-29 have adopted different family planning methods, while 98.20 per cent of married women in the age group of 40-44 have adopted family planning. Of course, the women belonging to the age group of 40-44 have a very short period of fertility, hence their share in birth control is very small. Table - 3.38 indicates various methods of family planning and their percentage adopted by eligible couples.

The rate of women who have adopted permanent family planning is ten times more than that of men. This clearly indicates that in our male dominated society men are yet not ready to get operated for various social reasons. Condoms are also less used, while oral pills are considered to be the safest method of family planning. It can be derived from the report that the Family Welfare Centres have successfully carried out their operations to achieve the goal of family planning but they have not succeeded in keeping the desired distance between two children.

### 3.22 Summary

The chapter attempts to discuss the socio-economic characteristics and demographic profile of India, Gujarat and Surat. Though the study area of this thesis is Surat it has been necessary to discuss the macro factors affecting population growth not only of the city but also of the state and the country, hence this chapter attempts to throw some light on these relevant macro factors as well. This has also been necessary to decide the place of Surat in the process of urbanization that has taken place both at the national and the state level. The primary information regarding census is made available by the Government machinery at regular intervals. These primary data have been used in discussing the socio-economic characteristics and the demographic profile of India, Gujarat, Surat. The chapter also attempts to discuss the total population and the changes in population that have taken place in India, Gujarat and Surat. The changes in birth rate, IMR, urbanization and occupational distribution have also been given consideration in the discussion. All the available information obtained from the primary data available from census 2001 have been included and discussed here.

The total population of India according to census 2001 primary data is 1,027,015247 and the population of Gujarat state is 50596992. Surat possesses the total population of 24,32,787. It is noticeable that at all these three levels – national, state and local – the female population is lower than male population. In each census period the rate of female population is going lower, which is a problem for sociologists. A remarkable decline has been noticed both in birth rate and death rate. IMR is also fast declining. In Surat birth rate is 20 while death rate is around 4.5 and IMR is 21.01. The available data of population of India, Gujarat and Surat are put together so that a comparative study of population at all three levels can be carried out and results can be arrived at.

It has also been observed in the present study that Gujarat is one of the high income states of India, hence its performance is better as far as socio-economic development is concerned. Compared to other states, Gujarat stands second to Maharashtra in the proportion of urban population (34.49 per cent) and Surat is positioned second in urban population in the state. Population growth is also more than other cities as people from outside continuously come to Surat in search of job. The distribution of population is based on occupational preferences. The main work force in the diamond industry is from Saurashtra while in textiles there are mainly people from U.P. and Orissa. The diversity of population and occupation based population distribution greatly affects population growth, hence these diverse effects on the population growth of Surat city is the main concern of this study.

**Table – 3.1**

**Population Growth in India**

| Census | Population (lakh) | Decade Increases | Percentage | Annual Growth rate |
|---|---|---|---|---|
| 1901 | 2384 | -- | -- | -- |
| 1911 | 2521 | +137 | +5.75 | 0.56 |
| 1921 | 2513 | -8 | -0.30 | -0.03 |
| 1931 | 2790 | +277 | +11.00 | 1.06 |
| 1941 | 3187 | +397 | +14.23 | 1.34 |
| 1951 | 3611 | +424 | +13.31 | 1.26 |
| 1961 | 4392 | +781 | +21,64 | 1.93 |
| 1971 | 5482 | +1090 | +24.80 | 2.24 |
| 1981 | 6852 | +1370 | +25.00 | 2.28 |
| 1991 | 8463 | +1611 | +23.50 | 2.14 |
| 2001 | 10270 | +1807 | +21.34 | 2.14 |

Source: Census Report, 1991

**Table – 3.2**

**Average Annual Birth Rate and Death Rate in India**

| Time | Annual Birth Rate | Annual Death Rate | Natural Increases |
|---|---|---|---|
| 1901-10 | 49.2 | 42.6 | 0.6 |
| 1911-20 | 48.1 | 48.6 | -0.5 |
| 1921-30 | 48.4 | 36.3 | 10.1 |
| 1931-40 | 45.2 | 31.2 | 14.0 |
| 1941-50 | 39.90 | 27.4 | 12.5 |
| 1951-60 | 41.7 | 22.8 | 18.9 |
| 1961-70 | 41.2 | 19.0 | 22.0 |
| 1971-80 | 37.2 | 15.0 | 22.2 |
| 1981-86 | 33.2 | 12.2 | 21.0 |
| 1986-1991 | 30.9 | 10.8 | 20.1 |

Source: Census Report 1991

**Table – 3.3**

**Density of Population in India**

| Years | Density |
|---|---|
| 1951 | 117 |
| 1961 | 142 |
| 1971 | 177 |
| 1981 | 216 |
| 1991 | 267 |
| 2001 | 324 |

Source: Census Report 1991 Provisional Population Totals 2001

**Table – 3.4**

**Sex Ratio of India (Per thousand males)**

| Years | Rural | Urban | India |
|---|---|---|---|
| 1901 | 979 | 910 | 972 |
| 1911 | 975 | 872 | 964 |
| 1921 | 970 | 846 | 955 |
| 1931 | 966 | 838 | 950 |
| 1941 | 965 | 831 | 945 |
| 1951 | 965 | 860 | 946 |
| 1961 | 963 | 845 | 941 |
| 1971 | 949 | 858 | 930 |
| 1981 | 951 | 879 | 934 |
| 1991 | 938 | 874 | 927 |
| 2001 | -- | -- | 933 |

Source: Census Report 1991 Provisional Population Totals Paper-II (Census-2001)

Table – 3.5

World Urban Population

| | As percentage of total population | | Average Annual Growth | | Percentage of Urban Population in a Cities of Millions or above | |
|---|---|---|---|---|---|---|
| | 1980 | 1994 | 1980-90 | 1990-94 | 1980 | 1994 |
| Law Income Economics | 22 | 28 | 4.2 | 3.8 | 32 | 34 |
| Middle Income Group | 52 | 61 | 3.0 | 2.4 | 32 | 33 |
| High Income Economics | 76 | 77 | 0.8 | 0.3 | 40 | 43 |
| India | 23 | 27 | 3.2 | 2.9 | 25 | 35 |

Source: World Development Report, 1996.

Table – 3.6

Trends of Urbanization of India

| Year | No. of A/S Towns | Size of Urban Population | Percentage Urban | Annual Growth |
|---|---|---|---|---|
| 1901 | 1827 | 25851873 | 10.84 | -- |
| 1951 | 2843 | 62443709 | 17.29 | -- |
| 1961 | 2365 | 78936003 | 17.97 | 2.34 |
| 1971 | 2590 | 1091113977 | 19.91 | 3.21 |
| 1981 | 3378 | 15946247 | 23.34 | 3.83 |
| 1991 | 3768 | 217611012 | 25.72 | 3.09 |

Source: Census of India, 1991

**Table – 3.7**

**Natural Increase Rate in India**

| | | Urban | Rural | Diff. between u/R |
|---|---|---|---|---|
| 1971-80 | Birth rate | 28.5 | 35.8 | -7.3 |
| | Death rate | 9.2 | 15.8 | -6.6 |
| | Natural Increase rate | 19.3 | 20.0 | -0.7 |
| 1981-90 | Birth rate | 27.3 | 34.2 | -6.7 |
| | Death rate | 7.7 | 12.8 | -5.1 |
| | Natural Increase rate | 19.6 | 21.4 | -1.8 |

Source: Census of India, 1991 Paper-2 of 1991, Provisional Population Total Rural/Urban Distribution Census as social Development Edited by Mohanthy & Amin P. 186.

**Table – 3.8**

**Components of Urban Population Growth Percentage Share in Urban Population Growth**

| Period | Rural to Urban | Area Reclassification |
|---|---|---|
| 1951-61 | 41.40 | 23.02 |
| 1961-71 | 18.87 | 18.23 |
| 1971-80 | 18.40 | 20.97 |

Source: Census of India, Occupational Paper-1 of 1988.

**Table – 3.9**

**Number of literate and illiterate among population (Aged Seven years and above – India 1981-91-2001 (In million)**

| | Persons | | Males | | Females | |
|---|---|---|---|---|---|---|
| | Lit. | Illiterate | Lit. | Illiterate | Lit. | Illiterate |
| 1981 | 234.257 | 302.063 | 137.084 | 120.96 | 77.07 | 126.10 |
| 1991 | 349.762 | 320.410 | 223.708 | 124.77 | 126.06 | 195.64 |
| 2001 | 562.011 | 296.209 | 335.970 | 106.654 | 225.041 | 199.555 |

Source: Census of India, 1991, series-I paper-2 of 1992, Final population total, Brief Analysis of Primary Absent Statement-14, Excluding Assam and J&K. Census of India, 2001, Provisional Population Totals Paper-1 of 2001, India.

**Table – 3.10**

**Literates Per Thousand**

| Year | Male | Female | Persons |
|---|---|---|---|
| 1901 | 98 | 7 | 54 |
| 1911 | 106 | 11 | 59 |
| 1921 | 122 | 18 | 72 |
| 1931 | 156 | 29 | 95 |
| 1941 | 249 | 73 | 141 |
| 1951 | 250 | 79 | 167 |
| 1961 | 344 | 130 | 240 |
| 1971 | 395 | 187 | 245 |
| 1981 | 469 | 248 | 362 |
| 1991 | 641 | 313 | 522 |
| 2001 | 759 | 542 | 654 |

Source: Office of the Registrar General, India, Vol. II 1991, P. 672. Census 2001, Provisional Report.

**Table – 3.11**

**Percentage of Literates by Age and Sex 1981-1991**

| Age Group | Males | Female | Percentage |
|---|---|---|---|
| **1981** | | | |
| 5-9 | 34.7 | 25.6 | 30.2 |
| 10-14 | 66.8 | 44.8 | 56.4 |
| 15-19 | 66.1 | 43.3 | 55.4 |
| 20-24 | 66.6 | 37.2 | 52.0 |
| 25-34 | 60.7 | 28.9 | 45.1 |
| 35+ Above | 44.7 | 14.5 | 30.3 |
| All ages | 44.9 | 24.8 | 36.2 |
| **1991** | | | |
| 5-9 | 62.6 | 51.0 | 56.9 |
| 10-14 | 77.0 | 59.7 | 68.8 |
| 15-19 | 75.3 | 54.9 | 65.8 |
| 20-24 | 71.6 | 43.8 | 57.8 |
| 25-34 | 64.7 | 36.6 | 50.8 |
| 35+ Above | 52.6 | 22.0 | 38.1 |
| All ages | 64.1 | 39.3 | 52.2 |

Source: Registrar General of India, Excludes Assam 1981, Excludes J&K, 1991.

**Table – 3.12**

**Percentage drop out in different stages of school education - 1991**

| | Boys | Girls |
|---|---|---|
| Primary | 40.10 | 45.97 |
| Middle | 59.12 | 65.13 |
| High School | 67.50 | 76.96 |

Source: Ministry of HRD Education in India.

**Table – 3.13**

**Fertility by Education and Religion**

| Religion | Hindu | Muslim |
|---|---|---|
| TFR | 3.30 | 4.41 |
| Illiterate | 3.93 | 5.03 |
| Less than Middle school | 2.93 | 3.61 |
| High school and above | 2.07 | 2.97 |
| Children ever born | 3.0 | 3.6 |
| Children Survival | 2.6 | 3.2 |

Source: NFHS, India 1998. EPW A Sameksha Trust Publication No. 42 and 43 October, 16-22/23 – 1999, P. 3049.

**Table – 3.14**

**IMR in India**

| Years | IMR |
|---|---|
| 1911-20 | 278 |
| 1951-60 | 140 |
| 1981 | 110 |
| 1991 | 80 |
| 1995 | 80 |
| 1996 | 77 |
| 1997 | 77 |
| 2010 | 30* |

Source: Registrar General Office (SRS), India.

* New Population Policy, Feb. 2000.

**Table – 3.15**

**IMR in Rural, Urban and India**

| Year | Rural | Urban | Combined |
|---|---|---|---|
| 1971 | 138 | 82 | 129 |
| 1976 | 139 | 80 | 129 |
| 1981 | 119 | 62 | 110 |
| 1986 | 105 | 62 | 96 |
| 1991 | 87 | 53 | 79 |
| 1996 | 77 | 46 | 72 |
| 1997 | 77 | 45 | 71 |

Source: Office of the Registrar General, India (SRS)

**Table – 3.16**

**Estimates of IMR and Child Mortality**

| | IMR | | CMR | |
|---|---|---|---|---|
| | M | F | M | F |
| 1981 | 110 | 111 | 39 | 43 |
| 1989 | 92 | 90 | 29 | 31 |
| 1992-93 | 88.6 | 83.9 | 29.4 | 42 |

Source: NFHS – 1992-03 IIPS, Mumbai.

**Table – 3.17**

**Expectation of Life at Birth by Sex in India**

| Year | Male | Female | Persons |
|---|---|---|---|
| 1901-11 | 22.6 | 23.3 | 22.9 |
| 1951-61 | 41.9 | 40.6 | 41.3 |
| 1961-71 | 47.1 | 45.6 | 46.3 |
| 1971-75 | 50.5 | 49.6 | 49.7 |
| 1981-85 | 55.4 | 55.7 | 55.4 |
| 1991-95 | 59.7 | 60.9 | 60.3 |

Source: Office of the Registrar General, India
(i) Census Actual Reports
(ii) Sample Registration System

**Table – 3.18**

**Total Population Growth in Gujarat**

| Year | Total Population Lakh | Decade Increase | Density |
|---|---|---|---|
| 1891-01 | 91 | -- | 46 |
| 1901-11 | 98 | +7.79 | 50 |
| 1911-21 | 102 | 3.79 | 52 |
| 1921-31 | 115 | 2.92 | 59 |
| 1931-41 | 137 | 19.25 | 70 |
| 1941-51 | 163 | 18.69 | 83 |
| 1951-61 | 206 | 26.88 | 105 |
| 1961-71 | 207 | 29.39 | 136 |
| 1971-81 | 341 | 27.67 | 174 |
| 1981-91 | 413 | 21.19 | 211 |
| 1991-2001 | 506 | 22.66 | 258 |

Source: Census of India, Final Population tables Series-1 India, Paper-1 of 1992
Census 2001, Provisional Population Tables, Paper-II, Gandhinagar.

**Table – 3.19**

**Rural and Urban Population in Gujarat (Population – Lakh)**

| Year | Total | Rural | Urban | Urban Percentage |
|---|---|---|---|---|
| 1961 | 206.33 | 153.17 | 53.160 | 25.76 |
| 1971 | 266.90 | 192.61 | 76.96 | 28.08 |
| 1981 | 340.86 | 234.84 | 106.02 | 31.10 |
| 1991 | 413.10 | 270.64 | 142.46 | 34.49 |
| 2001 | 483.87 | 301.60 | 182.27 | 37.67 |

Source: Census of India– 1991 Census 2001, Provisional population Totals Paper-II.
The figure exclude earthquake affected area of Kutch, Jamnagar, Rajkot.

**Table – 3.20**

**Total Population, Density and Sex ratio of Main Cities of Gujarat - 1991**

| Cities | Total | Density | Decant | Sex-ratio |
|---|---|---|---|---|
| Ahmedabad | 2676710 | 15402 | 23.47 | 889 |
| Surat | 1498817 | 13483 | 62.23 | 839 |
| Vadodara | 1031346 | 9527 | 40.42 | 899 |
| Rajkot | 559407 | 8107 | 25.69 | 930 |
| Bhavnagar | 402338 | 4462 | 31.00 | 927 |
| Jamnagar | 341637 | 12941 | 23.06 | 919 |
| Nadiad | 167051 | 5866 | 17.07 | 937 |
| Junagadh | 130484 | 9697 | 9.98 | 933 |
| Porbandar | 116671 | 9485 | 1.29 | 946 |
| Bharuch | 133102 | 7222 | 18.20 | 941 |

Source: Census of India, 1991

**Table – 3.21-A**

**Women Population (lakh) – 1991 in Gujarat**

| | Total | Male | Female |
|---|---|---|---|
| Rural | 270.64 | 138.85 | 131.79 |
| Urban | 142.46 | 74.71 | 67.75 |
| Total | 413.10 | 213.56 | 199.54 |

Source: Census Report – 1991

**Table – 3.21-B**

**Women Population (lakh) – 2001 in Gujarat**

| | Total | Male | Female |
|---|---|---|---|
| Rural | 301.60 | 155.06 | 146.53 |
| Urban | 182.27 | 97.02 | 85.25 |
| Total | 483.87 | 252.08 | 231.78 |

Source: Census 2001, Provisional Report (Excludes earthquake affected areas)

**Table – 3.22**

**Birth rate, Death rate and IMR – (Rural + Urban = Gujarat)**

| | Birth rate | | | Death rate | | | |
|---|---|---|---|---|---|---|---|
| **Year** | **Rural** | **Urban** | **Combined** | **Rural** | **Urban** | **Combined** | **IMR** |
| 1981 | 26.1 | 29.8 | 34.5 | 12.4 | 10.7 | 12 | 116 |
| 1991 | 28.2 | 25.9 | 27.5 | 8.8 | 7.9 | 8.5 | 69 |
| 1992 | 29.5 | 24.6 | 28.1 | 9.5 | 8.3 | 9.2 | 67 |
| 1993 | 29.5 | 25.8 | 28.0 | 8.9 | 6.8 | 8.2 | 58 |
| 1994 | 28.5 | 24.0 | 27.1 | 9.6 | 6.9 | 8.7 | 64 |
| 1995 | 27.9 | 24.6 | 26.7 | 8.3 | 6.2 | 7.6 | 62 |
| 1996 | 26.9 | 23.0 | 25.7 | 8.3 | 6.2 | 7.6 | 61 |

Source: Sample Registrar Bulletin, Registrar General India, Ministry of Home Affairs, New Delhi.
-- Commissioner of Health and Medical Services and Medical Education (Health), Gujarat state, Gandhinagar.

**Table – 3.23**

**Literacy Rate in Gujarat & India**

| **Years** | **Gujarat (%)** | **India (%)** |
|---|---|---|
| 1901 | 7.93 | 5.35 |
| 1911 | 9.12 | 5.92 |
| 1921 | 10.85 | 7.16 |
| 1931 | 11.98 | 9.50 |
| 1941 | NA | NA |
| 1951 | 21.69 | 10.69 |
| 1961 | 30.45 | 24.02 |
| 1971 | 35.79 | 29.46 |
| 1981 | 49.96 | 46.56 |
| 1991 | 61.29 | 52.51 |
| 2001 | 69.27 | 65.38 |

Source: Socio-Economic Review 1997-98, p. 18. (2) Census 2001, Primary Report

**Table – 3.24**

**Literacy in Gujarat (U/R)**

**1991–2001 (Numbers and Percentage)**

| | Numbers | | | Percentage | | |
|---|---|---|---|---|---|---|
| | Male | Female | Total | Male | Female | Total |
| Rural 1991 | 7680019 | 4227275 | 11907294 | 66.89 | 38.65 | 53.09 |
| Urban 1991 | 5345113 | 3878993 | 9224106 | 84.56 | 67.70 | 76.54 |
| Total 1991 | 13025132 | 8106268 | 21131400 | 73.13 | 48.64 | 61.29 |
| Rural 2001 | 9796390 | 6039979 | 15836369 | 74.95 | 48.52 | 62.05 |
| Urban 2001 | 7552789 | 5660861 | 13213650 | 89.01 | 75.30 | 82.57 |
| Total 2001 | 17349179 | 11700840 | 29050019 | 80.49 | 58.60 | 69.96 |

Source: Directorate of Census, Commissioner, Gujarat State, Ahmedabad.
2) Census of India, 2001, Provisional Population Totals Paper-2 of 2001, Gujarat.
Note: Excludes the children in the age group 0-6.

**Table – 3.25**

**Literacy Rate – Major Districts in Gujarat**

| | Total | Male | Female | Rural | Urban |
|---|---|---|---|---|---|
| Rajkot | 66.96 | 76.76 | 56.66 | 58.41 | 76.48 |
| Amreli | 60.06 | 71.26 | 48.77 | 56.85 | 71.69 |
| Junagadh | 60.33 | 72.41 | 47.83 | 54.99 | 71.35 |
| Uakasana | 65.14 | 78.0 | 51.61 | 61.86 | 76.57 |
| Gandhinagar | 87.11 | 93.21 | 80.51 | 86.62 | 87.82 |
| Ahmedabad | 73.11 | 82.73 | 62.39 | 55.12 | 78.94 |
| Kheda | 65.83 | 80.49 | 49.93 | 62.10 | 78.03 |
| Vadodara | 63.61 | 74.14 | 52.02 | 50.18 | 80.88 |
| Bharuch | 61.92 | 73.21 | 49.71 | 57.25 | 78.94 |
| Surat | 64.36 | 72.61 | 55.13 | 52.63 | 75.93 |
| Valsad | 64.35 | 73.48 | 54.79 | 59.01 | 80.56 |

Source: Census of India – 1991.

**Table – 3.26**

**Occupational Distribution of Population (Gujarat/India) – 1991**

| | Total (Percentage) | | Male (Percentage) | | Female (Percentage) | |
|---|---|---|---|---|---|---|
| | Gujarat | India | Gujarat | India | Gujarat | India |
| Primary | 59.8 | 67.5 | 54.5 | 63.1 | 81.7 | 81.2 |
| Secondary | 17.9 | 12.0 | 20.8 | 13.1 | 5.8 | 8.0 |
| Tertiary | 22.4 | 20.5 | 24.8 | 23.5 | 12.5 | 10.6 |

Source: Office of the Registrar General, India, Selected Socio-Economic Statistics, India, 1998, New Delhi, p. 88.

**Table – 3.27**

**Population Growth and Area – Expansion (1951-2001) Surat**

| **Year** | **Area (k.m.)** | **Decadal Variation in Population** | | |
|---|---|---|---|---|
| | | **Population** | **Absolute** | **Proportion** |
| 1951 | 8.18 | 237394 | -- | -- |
| 1961 | 24.01 | 317519 | +80.125 | +33.75 |
| 1971 | 49.37 | 471656 | +154117 | +48.54 |
| 1981 | 55.55 | 776583 | +304927 | +64.65 |
| 1991 | 111.55 | 1498817 | +722234 | +95.00 |
| 2001 | 112.28 | 2433787 | +934970 | +62.38 |

Source: Shah Ghanshyam, Public Health and Urban Develop in Surat 1997, Sage Publications, New Delhi, p. 47.
(2) Census 2001, Provisional Population Totals, Gandhinagar, Gujarat.

**Table – 3.28**

**Population and Density of Six Cities (MC Status) - Gujarat**

| Municipal Corporation | Population | Density |
|---|---|---|
| Ahmedabd | 3415361 | 18420 |
| Surat | 2433785 | 21676 |
| Vadodara | 1306035 | 12064 |
| Rajkot | 966642 | 9218 |
| Bhavnagar | 510958 | 5667 |
| Jamnagar | 443397 | 16871 |

Source: Census – 2001, Provisional Populations Totals, Paper-II, Gandhinagar, Gujarat.

**Table – 3.29**

**Density of Surat City**

| Year | Density |
|---|---|
| 1971 | 13954 |
| 1981 | 13977 |
| 1991 | 14818 |
| 2001 | 21676 |

Source: Census 2001, Provisional Report, Paper-II

**Table – 3.30**

**Density Inner and Inner Periphery Area**

| Years | Inner City zone Old city | Inner periphery and Rander zone | Other Zone |
|---|---|---|---|
| 1971<br>Populations<br>Density | <br>367703 (77%)<br>44462 | <br>107953 (23%)]<br>4214 | <br>--<br>-- |
| 1981<br>Populations<br>Density | <br>441325 (57%)<br>53952 | <br>335258 (43%)]<br>7076 | <br>--<br>-- |
| 1991<br>Populations<br>Density | <br>424352 (28%)<br>51876 | <br>644152 (43%)]<br>13598 | <br>4330312 (29%)<br>7739 |

Source: Ghosh Archana, Plague in Surat.
S. Sami Ahmed, Concept Publishing, 1996.

**Table – 3.31**

**Birth rate, Death rate and IMR in Surat (1991-2001)**

| Year | Birth | Death | IMR |
|---|---|---|---|
| 1991 | 29.95 | 5.5 | 23 |
| 1992 | 29.14 | 5.5 | 22.64 |
| 1993 | 23.24 | 4.80 | 21.67 |
| 1994 | 22.08 | 4.61 | 22.56 |
| 1995 | 23.26 | 4.29 | 22.11 |
| 1996 | 22.22 | 4.60 | 20.50 |
| 1997 | 22.65 | 4.29 | 18.99 |
| 1998 | 21.41 | 4.44 | 19.68 |
| 1999 | 21.62 | 4.24 | 22.27 |
| 2000 | 21.70 | 4.20 | 23.98 |
| 2001 | 22.01 | 4.20 | 21.01 |

Source: S.M.C. Health Department.

**Table – 3.32**

**Immunization Report (1999-2000) Surat**

| | Immunization | Target | Actual | Percentage |
|---|---|---|---|---|
| (1) | BCG | 61000 | 64497 | 105.83 |
| (2) | Polio | 61000 | 65851 | 107.95 |
| (3) | DTP | 61000 | 64919 | 106.42 |
| (4) | Measles | 61000 | 57624 | 94.48 |
| (5) | DT | 10000 | 14278 | 142.78 |
| (6) | T.T. (10 years) | 45500 | 9095 | 98.98 |
| (7) | T.T. (16 years) | 40500 | 8561 | 21.13 |
| (8) | G.T.T. | 67000 | 72349 | 107.00 |

Source: SMC, Health Department, Surat.

**Table – 3.33**

**Sex Ratio – Six Major Cities of Gujarat – 1961 - 2001**

| City | 1961 | 1971 | 1981 | 1991 | 2001 |
|---|---|---|---|---|---|
| Ahmedabad | 804 | 830 | 869 | 896 | 885 |
| Bhavnagar | 916 | 908 | 925 | 929 | 914 |
| Jamnagar | 907 | 913 | 916 | 936 | 904 |
| Rajkot | 927 | 920 | 925 | 925 | 907 |
| Surat | 921 | 884 | 840 | 839 | 774 |
| Vadodara | 856 | 852 | 889 | 898 | 904 |

Source: Census of India – 1971-1991, 2001 India.
Census 2001, Provisional Populations Totals, Paper-II, Gandhinagar.

**Table – 3.34**

**Literacy rate of Surat (1991-2001)**

| | Male | Female | Total |
|---|---|---|---|
| 1991 | 566882<br>(82.49%) | 385290<br>(68.05%) | 951872<br>(75.97%) |
| 2001 | 1054177<br>(88.41%) | 700588<br>(76.73%) | 1754765<br>(83.35%) |

Source: Census 2001, Provisional Population Totals, Paper-II, Gandhinagar.

**Table – 3.35**

**Estimated Population Distribution**

**Native and Migrant Population (Lakh)**

| | | |
|---|---|---|
| (i) | Saurastrians (Guj.) | 4 |
| (ii) | Oriyas | 4 |
| (iii) | Utter Pradesh, Bihar, A.P. Rajasthan, South India, Others | 8 |
| (iv) | Surat District | 4 |
| (v) | Suratis | 4 |
| | | **24 Lakh** |

Source: Amarendra Jha, Times of India.

**Table – 3.36**

**Distribution of Workers by Different Economic Activities in Surat - 1991**

| | Economic Activity | Population | Percentage |
|---|---|---|---|
| (i) | Cultivators | 2508 | 0.48 |
| (ii) | Agricultural labours | 4240 | 0.82 |
| (iii) | Livestock and Forestry | 2720 | 0.53 |
| (iv) | Mining and Quarring | 875 | 0.17 |
| (v) | Constructions | 17097 | 3.33 |
| (vi) | Manufacturing and Processing in house hold industry | 11325 | 2.21 |
| (vii) | Other than household industry | 283568 | 55.35 |
| (viii) | Trade and Commerce | 95844 | 18.70 |
| (ix) | Transport, Storage and Communication | 23028 | 4.49 |
| (x) | Other services | 67659 | 13.20 |
| (xi) | Marginal Worker | 3462 | 0.67 |
| Total | Worker | 512326 | 100.00 |
| | Total Non Worker | 986491 | 65.81 |
| | Total Population | 1498817 | 100.00 |

Source: Shah Ghanshyam, Public Health and Urban Development, The Plague in Surat, Sage Publications India Pvt. Ltd., New Delhi, 1997, p. 49.

**Table – 3.37**

**Age wise Family Planning Adopted by Eligible Women - 2002**

| Married women age | Different methods of F.P. Adopted | Not a Single Method Adopted | Eligible Couple |
|---|---|---|---|
| 15-19 | 10151 (51.10%) | 2609 (48.90%) | 12767 |
| 20-24 | 36389 (74.79%) | 12257 (25.21%) | 48646 |
| 25-29 | 48043 (91.52%) | 44453 (8.48%) | 52496 |
| 30-34 | 44039 (83.30%) | 8830 (16.70%) | 52869 |
| 35-39 | 37846 (87.53%) | 5391 (12.47%) | 43237 |
| 40-44 | 20662 (94.98%) | 1091 (5.02%) | 21753 |
| Total | 197137 (85.06%) | 34631 (14.94%) | 231768 |

Source: SMC, Urban Family Welfare Bureau Report 2002.

**Table – 3.38**

**Various Methods Adopted by Eligible Couples Surat - 2002**

| Methods | Couple (No) | Percentage |
|---|---|---|
| Vasectomy | 11616 | 5.89 |
| Tubectomy | 98594 | 50.01 |
| Copper-T | 47222 | 23.95 |
| Condom | 29168 | 14.80 |
| Oral Pills | 10537 | 5.35 |
| Total | 197137 | 100 |

Source: SMC, Urban Family Welfare Bureau, Report 2002.

# CHAPTER – IV
# RESEARCH METHODOLOGY

The present study seeks to examine the relationship between population growth and socio-economic factors at the household level. The study area – Surat city – has been chosen from the state of Gujarat, India. In this chapter, an attempt has been made to discuss the methods and materials used for the organisation of the study; i.e. conceptual frame work, definitions, area of the study, units of analyses, sample design and size, tools used for data collection, statistical techniques, pre-test and data analysis. The chapter also discuses socio-economic characteristics and demographic profile of the study.

## 4.1 Conceptual Framework

A modified conceptual framework has been developed for this study (fig. 4.1) based on the earlier conceptual models evolved by Mason (1984) and Mahadevan (1989), and through the literature available on the subject under consideration. From the earlier studies, it has been found that a number of socio-economic and demographic factors like religion, migration, marital status, level of education, household income, work status of individuals, the occupational pattern in the family as well as in the urban area etc. do affect

**Figure – 4.1**
**Conceptual Framework Population Growth – Determinants**

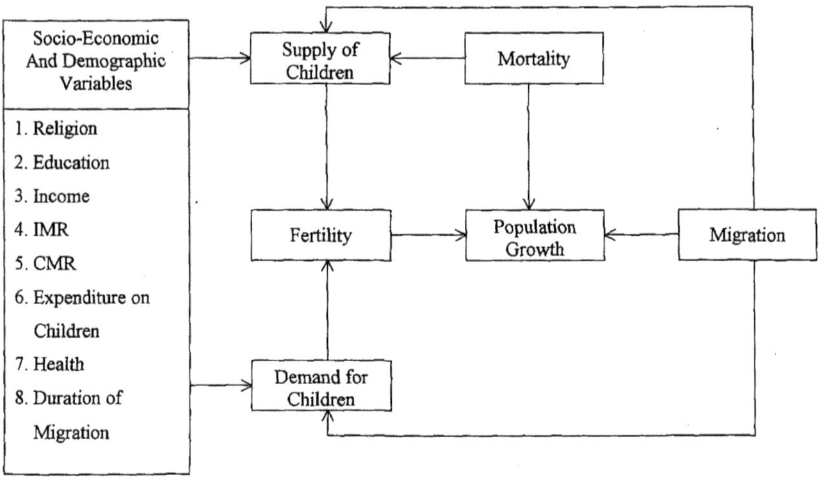

the decision making regarding number of children. Hence these variables are the status affecting variables (SAVs). These factors have their influence on fertility behaviour, directly as well as indirectly.

Higher education, socio-economically sound situation and better position at household level have further provided access to and control over economic resources and have encouraged greater participation of household.

It has been shown by numerous studies that population growth is affected by mortality, fertility and migration in urban area. Migration also indirectly affects fertility. Supply of children and demand for children are also factors affecting fertility. On the other hand, supply of children is affected by mortality. These three factors affect population growth, directly as well as indirectly. Some of the demographic variables – religion, marital status, level of education, household income etc. are also responsible for creating demand for and supply of children.

It has been normally observed that women and men who have higher educational level and economic independence value their sons and daughters equally. Moreover, such parents are likely to plan about the future of their children (quality of children) and thereby restrain themselves from the quantity of children. Thus, the level of education and economic independence considerably affect both demand for and supply of children.

## 4.2 Definition of Population Growth and its Determinants

Population growth is a continuous process. The fertility, mortality and migration are three main determinants of population growth. These determinants provide scope for population studies both at micro level and macro level. The size, composition and distribution of population are determined by births, deaths and migrations. The components of population changes are known as demographic variables. These variables are affected by socio-economic factors, which become the study area of demography.

Socio-economic factors play a vital role in population growth as they affect both the demand for and supply of children. Supply of children is influenced by natural fertility. Natural fertility is determined by the following factors:

(i) The duration of postpartum infecund ability.

(ii) Fecund ability (natural)

(iii) The risk of intra-uterine mortality

(iv) The onset of permanent sterility.

Demand for children is multi-dimensional, i.e. number, gender and spacing of surviving children. Major considerations for demand are, (i) children as economic asset and old age security, (ii) emergence of conjugal family, (iii) weakening of cultural property for high fertility and (iv) rising ambitions of parents.

### 4.3 Universe of the Study

The nature of the problem and the required variables naturally demand for a micro level empirical investigation, especially with urban households as the units of analysis. Hence, it was decided to conduct this study in an urban area of Gujarat. However, given the resource and time constraints, it was felt that covering the entire urban area would not be possible. Hence, it was decided to restrict the scope of the study to Surat city in Gujarat, India. Surat is found to be desirable in terms of greater accessibility to the investigator in time, money and energy. Surat is a fast expanding industrial city with deep-rooted cultural values. It is known as 'The Diamond City', 'The Textile City', and 'The Green and Clean City' in the last couple of years of its growth. This shows that Surat is an ever-changing city, where people are heterogeneous in nature. People residing here, socio-economically belong to upper, middle and lower middle classes.

### 4.4 Units of Analysis

The present study is based on primary data. Households were selected as units of analysis.

**A Brief Discussion of the Study Area**

***1. Geographical Expansion***

Surat is an expanding city. During the last twenty-seven years, the area of the city has almost doubled. In the year 1975, the area of Surat was 55.56

square kilometers. At present, the city occupies 111.16 square kilometers (SMC). This expansion has merged the surrounding villages like Nana Varachha, Majura, Bamroli, Udhana, Bhedvad, Dindoli, Limbayat, Anjana, Umarvada, Dumbhal, Magob, Jahangirabad and Jahangirpura into SMC Limits. These demographic transitions provide a good scope for the study of socio-economic characteristics of the city and also of the trends of population growth.

*2. Expansion of Industries*

(i) The textile, diamond and Zari industries have played a major role in the present development of the city. The textile industry provides maximum employment to the people. Second comes the diamond industry.

(ii) Due to large employment opportunities available in the city, people from all over the country constantly pour into the city, changing the demographic profile of the place. During the last fifteen years the coastal belt of Hazira has undergone a sea-change, as large industries like Larsen and Toubro, ONGC, Reliance Petro-Chemicals and Reliance Textiles, ESSAR Steel, KRIBHCO etc. have been established.

(iii) These large-scale business units have attracted educated masses from all corners of the country to come to Surat. These migrants have been instrumental in bringing about remarkable changes in the socio-economic and cultural structure of the city.

(iv) Majority of the population migrated from outside Surat happen to be from the surrounding villages on the outskirts of the city. These villages are economically well off because of rich, fertile agricultural land good facilities of irrigation available to almost all villages. This means the push factors are not very important for the migration from the surrounding villages, but it is the pull factors, which seems to be responsible for this migration.

(a) It has been observed that the people migrating to Surat from the various corners of the country prefer to live in particular areas only, e.g. people from Saurashtra are pocketed in the Varachha area while rich Marvaris and Hariyanvi-Punjabis live in the posh areas of Bhatar and Athwa Lines. Maharashtrians, Oriyas, Biharis reside in the areas like Udhana, Bamroli, Bhestan. The service class people from the different parts of the country are found in the western part of the city, providing this area a cosmopolitan appearance. These migratory people have changed the socio-cultural scenario of the areas in which they live. It is interesting to note that they have brought a remarkable change in the habits and language of the local population. This factor might have same bearing.

(b) The total population of Surat at present is around 25 lakh. In 1991, it was just around 15 lakh. During 1971-81 the population growth of the city was 85.35 per cent. During the last decade the growth of population has been 62.37 per cent. Though the rate of population has decreased during the last decade, the total population has increased. This has provided a good model for the study of demographic changes that have taken place in the city.

The above-cited characteristics of the region have provided the base for understanding this study on Surat.

### 4.5 Sampling Design and Size

In the sample area – Surat city – the study samples were selected from the households spread over 33 wards of the city. The researcher intended to collect information from 450 households using cluster-sampling technique from the entire study area spread over 33 wards. From these ward no. 1, 8, 16, 24 and 32 were selected based on simple random equal-distance sampling technique, wherein 450 households were enumerated as per voters' list. From the above-mentioned wards, samples were selected at random. On scrutiny it was found that 26 households did not provide relevant information or inadequate information. They are discarded from the analyses.

### 4.6 Tools Used for Data Collection

Keeping the objectives of the study in mind schedule was prepared to collect the information. Most of the entries in the interview schedule are structured and close-ended questions. The interview schedule consists of questions about the head of the household, about the native place of the family and other details of the members of the household. The information about educational level, mortality rate, fertility rate, family planning, children preferences, family condition and family type, expenditure on health, education etc. were collected. Data for the present study were collected personally by the investigator between August 2001 and December 2001.

### 4.7 Pre-Test

A draft interview schedule was gone through by some experts in the field and their suggestions were incorporated. Then a pre test was done with 10 schedules and on the basis of the pre test results, the interview schedule was modified and further developed. A copy of the finalised interview schedule is given in the Appendix. The questions in the schedule were included after detailed discussion and analysis with the experts in this field.

### 4.8 Analysis of Data (Statistical Analysis)

After collection of the data, they were meticulously edited and all the informations were crosschecked carefully. The data were transferred on to code sheets and there after they were stored on a floppy disk. The preliminary analysis of the data was carried out in terms of frequency distribution and cross tabulations. For this purpose the statistics used were mostly percentages and averages. Religion, native and migrated population, durable goods of households, housing conditions, fertility behaviour of women, children ever born, desired family size, use of contraception etc. form the dependent variables for most of the analysis. These analyses helped to understand some other aspects of population growth; i.e. fertility, mortality and migration. Mortality affects supply of children, value of child survival, IMR and child mortality. These were treated as dependent variables. Demand for children was treated as an independent variable, and the total number of children was treated as central variable throughout the preliminary analysis.

The final stage of analysis was carried out on the basis of the conceptual framework described earlier. For this purpose analysis was employed taking into consideration total number of children per household by different variables like children ever born, desired family size, IMR, child mortality and migrant people's demographic behaviour etc. In this process zero-order correlations and a series of multiple regression equations were estimated. On the other hand, logic analysis was used to assess the magnitude of each of the explanatory variables under consideration on family planning and immunization practices. The details of these techniques are highlighted in the sections concerned.

## 4.9 Socio-Economic Characteristics and Demographic Discipline of Sample Households

Before discussing the finding with respect to the influence of population growth and its related determinants and other related aspects, a brief examination of the socio-economic and demographic characteristics of the households is of vital importance.

The socio-economic characteristics taken into consideration include religion, native, household asset, housing condition, migration, income, expenditure, fertility, mortality, health, immunization, occupational status, status of the household, marital status, age at marriage of the couple, duration of their married life and the spousal age difference etc. These are treated here as the demographic characteristics. Apart from the above mentioned characteristics, fertility behaviour in terms of number of children ever born, gender, the rate of child survival and the desired family size are also discussed here. The information on migration characteristics, family planning details, health variables, immunization record and parental preferences is also presented.

## 4.10 Socio-Economic Characteristics

### (i) *Religion*

Religion is one of the important socio-cultural factors in India. In the sample population (Table - 4.1), an overwhelming proportion of the households are Hindus (88.4 per cent), whereas only a small proportion is Muslims (7.8%) and others (3.8%). Caste is another important socio-cultural factor. But in this study caste is not taken into consideration. Instead of caste classification, households have been classified by income level groups in the sample population of the study (Table - 4.2).

(ii) ***Place of Birth***

The study has been conducted only in the urban area, wherein majority of the respondents (72.9%) were born in Surat and the remaining (27.1%) were those who were born outside Surat and eventually migrated to Surat (Table - 4.1).

(iii) ***Family Type***

The predominant family types observed in the sample population were joint families and single families. The joint family consists of husband, wife and married children, whereas the single family consists of husband, wife and unmarried children. Joint families were more common (50%) in the study area, whereas the proportion of single families was 30.4% and a small proportion – 19.1% of the households – consisted of nuclear families.

(iv) ***Educational Status***

The sample population indicates the level of education of the heads of households (Table - 4.1). This indicates highest education of women. 27.45

per cent women are just literate, 20.34 per cent have obtained primary education, 41.18 per cent have reached up to high school and higher secondary and 11.03 per cent have obtained higher education (bachelor's degree and above). These data will be helpful in finding relationship between total number of children in a family and the level of education.

### 4.11 Economic Characteristics of the Sample Households

Based on economic conditions, occupations of households have been broadly classified into eight categories; i.e., manufacturers, industrials (organized), industrials (unorganized), ordinary labourers, services, business, agents and self employed (Table - 4.2). Samples are taken from different parts of Surat city area. The occupational distribution of the households reveal that 9.2 per cent of households are manufacturers, followed by nearly less than one fourth (21.5 per cent) in business, textiles and diamonds, and small scale industries owners and 14.2 per cent are self-employed households. Slightly more than one half – 54.17 per cent – are engaged in services, i.e., clerical and related white-collar pursuits, inclusive of ordinary labourers.

The sample households are further divides into four categories: ordinary, industrial, non-industrial and mixed households. Out of 424 sample households 17.9 per cent (Table - 4.2) are engaged in ordinary occupations. In this category those people are included who do not have permanent source of income but are engaged on temporary basis or those who are under-employed especially in the fields of textile processing units, construction, security services etc. 10.6 per cent are engaged in industries, inclusive of manufacturers, both organized and unorganized, 33.3 per cent are engaged in non-industrial occupations, mainly service class people; i.e. white collar jobs and all administrative categories and technicians, while 38.2 per cent belong to mixed occupational category. This category includes households with service and self-employed workers. There are several families in Surat under this category. Some members of the family are engaged in the family owned weaving units while some are engaged in services. This is found to be a very common feature in the households who are natives of Surat.

The characteristics of the sample households indicate that the annual income of 1.4 per cent of the total households is less than Rs.10,000 per annum while the annual income of 5.9 per cent households is between Rs.1,00,000 and Rs.25,000, 44.8 per cent households earn between Rs.50,000 and Rs.10,000 annually. This means a little less than 50 per cent of households come under the category of middle-income group. Most of the households under this group belong to the mixed occupational category where the earning members of the households are engaged both in family owned business or industry and services. 20.7 per cent of the households' annual income falls between Rs.1 lakh and more. The results clearly indicate that the average economic condition of the people of Surat is better than other cities of Gujarat.

It has been found that in 68.2 per cent households, there is only one earning member, while in 20.8 per cent households there are two earning members. There are three earning members in 8.5 per cent households and four and five earning members in 2.4 per cent, and 0.2 per cent households respectively. In the 68.2 per cent households, there is only one earning member. The households can be categorised under two distinct classes; i.e. those families who belong to lower middle income group and those who belong to higher income group; earning more than 2 lakh per annum.

### 4.12 Household Asset

In the sample, households household asset are classified under three categories: (1) Primary needs, (2) Secondary requirements and (3) Luxury items. The classification of possession of durable household asset is a good indicator for measuring the individual household's standard of living. A glance at Table - 4.3 indicates that a good proportion (38.31 per cent) of the households are in possession of costly goods generally considered as luxurious items like scooter, car, television, refrigerator, washing machine, telephone, computers + internet etc. Out of these 38.31 per cent households there are only 14 per cent of households who possess cars and electronic gadgets, 46 per cent – just a little less than one half – of the households possess primary and secondary necessities like moped, scooter, fan, television, radio, refrigerator etc. The remaining 14.01 per cent have bicycle, moped, fan and radio. 3.8 per cent households also possess autorikshaws for commercial purposes:

### 4.13 Housing Condition

The following information of the housing condition is gathered from the sample survey of 424 households; Lighting, sanitation, drinking water, source of water, number of rooms in the house and the housing material used for construction of the walls, roof, floor etc. This information is put together under type of houses. On the basis of ownership, they are further divided into two types – ownership houses and rented houses. As Surat is expanding, the problem of housing is acute in the city. The population growth rate of the city is 6.6 per cent and the demand for residential units goes on increasing day by day. Initially the migrants have to accommodate themselves in the rented houses and gradually they become owners. The data on housing are summersied in table 4.4. About 12.5 per cent of households have rented houses whereas 86.8 per cent families in Surat have their own houses.

Based on the types of households, the accommodations are classified as huts, Kuchcha, Pukka and mixed type accommodations. The types of houses classified as above are based on the building materials used in the construction of walls, roof and floor. The 18.9 per cent of accommodations are huts or Kuchcha houses and 5.7 per cent are mixed type, while 75.5 per cent of houses in Surat are Pukka.

The condition of over population does affect both health as well as the quality of life of the people. The number of rooms of the individual households is used as a simple indicator of the over crowded condition of the city. On average, there are 2.55 persons per room in Surat. A majority of households – 56.8 per cent – possess one or two rooms. However, 33.5 per cent of households have three room accommodations and only 9.7 per cent possess four or more than four rooms.

The source of water and especially the drinking water, separate kitchen, separate sanitation facilities are important determinants of the health status of the members of the households and especially of the health of children. 64.6 per cent of households get piped water for drinking from public taps and 29.2 per cent of households have private pipe/taped water facility. A majority of households – 60.6 per cent – get drinking water from outside their houses. 68.2 per cent of households have separate sanitation and 78.3 per cent of households have separate kitchen.

### 4.14 Demographic Characteristics

The total number of both males and females of the sample population is 2080 out of which there are 1101 males and 979 females. The majority of respondents in the sample population are in the age group of 26-40 (50.60 per cent females and 49.40 per cent males) at the time of survey. This is followed by the respondents in the age group of 16-25 (47.23 per cent females and

50.77 per cent males). This shows that quite a large majority of respondents are in their reproductive age. Both the above-mentioned groups include almost half of the sample population. 42.65 per cent females and 57.35 per cent males are in the age group of 41-60, while 46.63 per cent females and 53.37 per cent males are in the age group of 7-15. These findings will be helpful in finding the sex ratio and dependency ratio of the sample population.

Out of the total sample, population 829 respondents were married at the time of survey. 49.45 per cent males and 50.55 per cent females were married. The average age of the respondents at marriage was 21.51 per cent. The average age of females at the time of marriage was 19.52 per cent and 23.54 per cent was the age at marriage of the male respondents. In sample results 24.58 per cent females and 7.56 per cent males were married before they obtained legally acceptable age of marriage.

Duration of marriage is another prominent variable in the demographic analysis. The details of duration of married life of the sample respondents indicates that about 8.5 per cent of them experienced less than five years, 8.7 per cent had 6 to 10 years duration and 9 per cent had lived 11 to 15 years of married life. A little less than one half of the population had lived 16 to 30 years of married life and 19 per cent lived more than 30 years of their married life. The mean duration of marital life of the respondents of the study area is 13.18 years.

Duration of marriage is another prominent variable in the demographic analysis. The details of duration of married life of the sample respondents indicates that about 8.5 per cent of them experienced less than five years, 8.7 per cent had six to ten years duration and 9 per cent had lived 11 to 15 years of married life. A little less than one half of the population had lived 16 to 30 years of married life and 19 per cent lived more than 30 years of married life. The mean duration of marital life of the respondents of the study area is 13.18 years.

In India it is very common that the husbands are older in age compared to their wives. This has been confirmed in study area, wherein the mean spousal age difference works out to be 4.16 years. Majority of the female respondents – 75.5 per cent – are younger by 3 to 5 years than their husbands. Further, the details reveal that the spousal age difference is 6 to 7 years in the case of 14.36 per cent of the respondents and 8 to 10 years of age difference is found in 8.42 per cent of respondents. In case of very small number – 1.73 per cent – of respondents, the husbands are older by 11 and more years than their wives.

### 4.15 Children Ever Born, Children Surviving and Desired Family Size

The distribution of respondents by children ever born and surviving number of children and the desired family size is presented in table 4.6. The mean of children ever born is quite low, 2.22, in the study area. It is to be noted here that this is not the completed family size of the respondents but it is the cumulative fertility of the respondents at the time of survey. 37.92 per cent of respondents gave birth to two children, while 21.50 per cent gave birth to three children and 16.90 per cent gave birth to one child only. 14.43 per cent of respondents gave birth to a large number of children, i.e. four children 8.22 per cent, five children 4.59 per cent, six seven and eight children 1.45 per cent. The mean of surviving children is only a little lower – 2.19 – than the mean children ever born; i.e. by 0.03 births. The fact that most of the children have survived up to the date of survey indicates that the level of IMR and child mortality is very low in Surat.

The fertility information obtained in the survey does not refer to completed fertility. As an alternative, information about the desired family size has been obtained from the sample households by asking them a question: "*According to you what is the ideal family size (persons)*?" The desired number of persons obtained from their responses is treated here as the desired family size. The mean desired family size is 4.27 (persons) in the study area.

## 4.16 Migration

The credit for making Surat a cosmopolitan city goes to its migrant population, which is 27.1 per cent. A little more than 50 per cent of them – 56.7 per cent – have migrated to Surat either for higher income or to improve their economic condition. Most of the migrants – 59.13 per cent – have shifted to Surat with family as permanent residents. The average number of children born before the families migrated to Surat is 2.24 and after migration is 2.16. The total number of migrants in the sample population is 115, out of which 27.83 per cent are temporary migrants, while 72.17 per cent households are permanent migrants. Those households residing in Surat for more than twenty-five years are not considered as migrants.

### 4.17 Family Planning

People are generally found to be more aware of the family planning programmes in urban areas compared to rural areas. The results of the sample population also indicate that more than 90 per cent (92.2 per cent) of the sample population is aware of family planning, 92 per cent believe in family planning, while 76.6 per cent of them have adopted family planning. Those who have adopted family planning have come to know about the various methods of family planning – both temporary and permanent – from various sources. The role of family physicians and primary health clinics is very important in bringing about awareness regarding family planning among the people. 41.54 per cent of households have obtained information about family planning from their family doctors, while 36.92 per cent of them have been made aware by the primary health clinics. The other important sources for family planning awareness are media, health workers and husband/wife.

61.23 per cent of couples have adopted permanent family planning, while 38.77 per cent have opted for temporary sterilization. Temporary methods of sterilization include condoms (45.24 per cent), oral pills (22.22 per cent) and copper T (19.84 per cent). In our male dominated society still men are not ready for sterlization. This is evident even in the results of sample population. 95.48 per cent of women have undergone sterlization operations, while only a small number – just 4.52 per cent – of men have been vasectomised. Most of those who have undergone family planning operations have opted for private clinics for such operations (62.31 per cent), while a small minority (2.01 per cent) have sought the help of medical camps organized either by the Government agencies or non-Government organizations.

### 4.18 Health and Immunization

Our national health policy places a major emphasis on ensuring health care by the year 2000. Birth rate, death rate, expenditure on health and the success of immunization programmes are the major indicators of success or failure of the health programmes. In the study area birth rate was 16.35, while death rate was 4.33. 22 female children and 12 male children were born in the last year as against the death of five female children and four male children. The mean of total expenditure on health per household was Rs. 1467.

The results of the sample population indicate (Table - 4.10) that the majority of people in the city (90.3 per cent of households) are aware of the immunization programmes, while a small minority (9.7 per cent households) is unaware of the need of immunization. Generally a record book is provided by doctors and health care centres to all the parents but 5.4 per cent did not care to keep record of their children's immunization, while 80.4 per cent maintained this record. The International Polio Eradication Programme is successfully carried out in the study area. 66.5 per cent of children were covered under this programme. Though Government run primary health centers provide facilities for immunization, people prefer to take the services of private clinics (54.2 per cent).

### 4.19 Parental Preferences

In the study, population the average number of children is 2.22. This is a clear indicator that the family planning programmes have succeeded in the urban areas to a greater extent and parents prefer quality children to quantity of children. The success of health programmes – especially immunization and sterilization – has reduced IMR and child mortality rate. People in the study area prefer to live in single-nuclear family as against joint or extended family. Naturally, they can take better care or wish to take better care of their children. For a little less than one half of the sample households (46.5 per cent), the education of children is not burdensome while a small number of households (11.3 per cent) find it to be highly burdensome. Most of the parents are unable to provide extra facilities like separate study, study aid equipments or vehicles to their children (63.4 per cent) but if they could, 27.8 per cent would like to provide such facilities to their male children, while only 5.7 per cent of them would provide these facilities to their female children. 38.3 per cent of parents want their male children to study above graduation, while 26.5 per cent want their daughters to go for higher studies, i.e. above graduation. The pattern clearly indicates that still people prefer to have male children in the family.

### 4.20 Summary

In the study samples the majority of households are Hindus. A large number of households are residents of Surat proper and live in single or nuclear families. The maximum education in the majority of households of sample population is up to highschool level. Majority of households are in the non-industrial occupation category. Only a few households have annual income which falls below poverty line. The majority of households earn an average income of Rs. 60,000 per annum.

The mean ages of men and women are 27.80 and 27.16 respectively, whereas the ages at marriage for them are 23.54 and 19.52 years respectively. The mean marital duration experienced by the sample population is 13.18 years, while the mean spousal age difference is 4.16 years, which is found to be a common pattern in the Indian context. Among the sample population the mean number of children ever born, children survival and the desired family size are 2.22, 2.20 and 4.27 respectively. Thus, it can be concluded that the two children norm – popularized both by the Government of India and non-Government/social organizations engaged in health and family welfare programmes – is universally accepted by the study population.

The sample population is located in an urban area and therefore, more than 90 per cent of families are aware of family planning, while a large majority – 76 per cent – have adopted permanent methods of family planning. The immunization figures also indicate that people are aware of such programmes and majority of them believe in quality of children, hence opt for two children in the family.

## TABLE – 4.1

### Social Characteristics (Household Samples)

(1)

| Religion | No. | Per cent |
|---|---|---|
| Hindu | 375 | 88.4 |
| Muslim | 33 | 7.8 |
| Others | 16 | 3.8 |
| **Total** | **424** | **100** |

(2)

| Residence | No. | Per cent |
|---|---|---|
| Native | 309 | 72.9 |
| Migrant | 115 | 27.1 |
| **Total** | **424** | **100** |

(3)

| Family Type | No. | Per cent |
|---|---|---|
| Single/Nuclear | 210 | 49.5 |
| Joint | 212 | 50.0 |
| Extended | 2 | 0.5 |
| **Total** | **424** | **100** |

(4) **Education (Highest)**

| Sr. No | Education | Head of the Household | | Household Women's | | Household | |
|---|---|---|---|---|---|---|---|
| | | No. | % | No. | % | No. | % |
| (1) | Ilit, Lit, and Lit with Schooling | 118 | 27.8 | 112 | 27.45 | 31 | 7.3 |
| (2) | Up to Primary | 87 | 20.5 | 83 | 20.34 | 48 | 11.3 |
| (3) | High School Higher Secondary | 167 | 39.4 | 168 | 41.18 | 224 | 52.8 |
| (4) | College and above | 52 | 12.3 | 45 | 11.03 | 111 | 28.5 |
| | **Total** | **424** | **100** | **408** | **100** | **424** | **100** |

**TABLE – 4.2**

**Economic Characteristics (Household Samples)**

**(1) Occupation of Household**

| **Occupation** | **No.** | **Percentage** |
|---|---|---|
| Manufacturer | 48 | 9.2 |
| Service | 224 | 54.1 |
| Business | 88 | 21.5 |
| Self-employment | 64 | 15.2 |
| **Total** | **424** | **100** |

**(2) Occupational Status**

| **Occupation** | **No.** | **Percentage** |
|---|---|---|
| Ordinary | 76 | 17.9 |
| Industrial | 45 | 10.6 |
| Non-Industrial | 141 | 33.3 |
| Mixed | 162 | 38.2 |
| **Total** | **424** | **100** |

**(3) Total Income (Rs.)**

| **Income** | **No.** | **Percentage** |
|---|---|---|
| < 10,000 | 6 | 1.4 |
| 10,001 – 25,000 | 25 | 5.9 |
| 25,001 – 50,000 | 115 | 27.1 |
| 50,001 – 1 lac | 190 | 44.8 |
| 1 lac – 2 lac | 79 | 18.6 |
| Above 2 lac | 9 | 2.1 |
| **Total** | **424** | **100** |

**(4) Number of Earning Members**

| **No.** | **Household** | **Percentage** |
|---|---|---|
| 1 | 289 | 68.2 |
| 2 | 88 | 20.8 |
| 3 | 36 | 8.5 |
| 4 | 10 | 2.4 |
| 5 | 1 | 0.2 |
| **Total** | **424** | **100** |

**TABLE – 4.3**

**Household Asset**

**(1) Vehicles:**

| Bicycle | No. | Percent |
|---|---|---|
| No | 191 | 45.0 |
| Yes | 233 | 55.0 |
| **Total** | **424** | **100** |

| Moped | No. | Percent |
|---|---|---|
| No | 325 | 76.7 |
| Yes | 99 | 23.3 |
| **Total** | **424** | **100** |

| Scooter | No. | Percent |
|---|---|---|
| No | 279 | 65.8 |
| Yes | 145 | 34.2 |
| **Total** | **424** | **100** |

| Car | No. | Percent |
|---|---|---|
| No | 406 | 95.8 |
| Yes | 18 | 3.8 |
| **Total** | **424** | **100** |

**(2) Entertainment:**

| Radio | No. | Percent |
|---|---|---|
| No | 354 | 83.5 |
| Yes | 70 | 16.5 |
| **Total** | **424** | **100** |

| Tape with Radio | No. | Percent |
|---|---|---|
| No | 239 | 56.4 |
| Yes | 185 | 43.6 |
| **Total** | **424** | **100** |

| Television | No. | Percent |
|---|---|---|
| No | 64 | 15.1 |
| Yes | 360 | 84.9 |
| **Total** | **424** | **100** |

| VCR | No. | Percent |
|---|---|---|
| No | 395 | 93.2 |
| Yes | 29 | 6.8 |
| **Total** | **424** | **100** |

| Music System | No. | Percent |
|---|---|---|
| No | 406 | 95.8 |
| Yes | 18 | 4.2 |
| **Total** | **424** | **100** |

## TABLE – 4.4

## Housing Condition

**(1) Ownership:**

| | No. | Percent |
|---|---|---|
| Owned | 368 | 86.8 |
| Rented | 56 | 13.2 |
| **Total** | **424** | **100** |

**(2) Type of House**

| | No. | Percent |
|---|---|---|
| Hut | 13 | 3.1 |
| Kuchha | 67 | 15.8 |
| Pukka | 320 | 75.5 |
| Mixed | 24 | 5.7 |
| **Total** | **424** | **100** |

**(3) Rooms**

| No. of Rooms | No. | Percent |
|---|---|---|
| 1 | 82 | 19.3 |
| 2 | 159 | 37.5 |
| 3 | 142 | 33.5 |
| 4-7 | 41 | 9.7 |
| **Total** | **424** | **100** |

**(4) Separate Kitchen:**

| | No. | Percent |
|---|---|---|
| No | 92 | 21.7 |
| Yes | 332 | 78.3 |
| **Total** | **424** | **100** |

**(5) Separate Sanitation:**

| | No. | Percent |
|---|---|---|
| No | 134 | 31.8 |
| Yes | 289 | 68.2 |
| **Total** | **424** | **100** |

**(6) Drinking Water:**

| | No. | Percent |
|---|---|---|
| With in | 166 | 39.1 |
| Out side | 258 | 60.8 |
| **Total** | **424** | **100** |

**(7) Source of Water:**

| | No. | Percent |
|---|---|---|
| Borewell | 27 | 5.8 |
| Personal | 124 | 29.2 |
| Public | 275 | 64.8 |
| **Total** | **424** | **100** |

**(8) Lighting:**

| | No. | Percent |
|---|---|---|
| Electric | 409 | 96.5 |
| Kerosene | 15 | 3.5 |
| **Total** | **424** | **100** |

## TABLE – 4.5

### Demographic Characteristics

**(1) Agewise Samples Population**

| Age | Female | Male | Total |
|---|---|---|---|
| 0-6 | 96 (46.60) | 110 (53.40) | 206 (100%) |
| 7-15 | 152 (46.63) | 174 (53.37) | 326 (100%) |
| 16-25 | 256 (47.23) | 286 (52.77) | 542 (100%) |
| 26-40 | 292 (50.60) | 285 (49.40) | 577 (100%) |
| 41-60 | 148 (42.45) | 199 (57.35) | 347 (100%) |
| $61^{+}$ | 35 (42.68) | 47 (57.32) | 82 (100%) |
| **Total** | **976 (47.07)** | **1101 (52.93)** | **2080 (100%)** |

**(2) Age at Marriage**

| Age | Female | Male | Total |
|---|---|---|---|
| $0 \leq 17$ | 4 | 103 | 107 |
| 18-19 | 27 | 140 | 167 |
| 20-21 | 84 | 98 | 182 |
| 22-23 | 100 | 43 | 143 |
| 24-25 | 99 | 22 | 121 |
| 26-30 | 80 | 10 | 90 |
| $31^{+}$ | 16 | 3 | 19 |
| **Total** | **410** | **419** | **829** |

**(3) Duration of Marriage**

| Years | No | Percent |
|---|---|---|
| $0 < 5$ | 46 | 8.5 |
| 6-10 | 47 | 8.7 |
| 11-15 | 48 | 9.0 |
| 16-20 | 31 | 24.4 |
| 21-30 | 102 | 19.3 |
| $31^{+}$ | 29 | 5.4 |
| **Total** | **404** | **100** |

**(4) Spousal Age Differential**

| Years | No | Percent |
|---|---|---|
| 0-3 | 155 | 38.37 |
| 4-5 | 150 | 37.13 |
| 6-7 | 58 | 14.36 |
| 8-10 | 34 | 8.42 |
| $11^{+}$ | 7 | 1.72 |
| **Total** | **404** | **100** |

**TABLE – 4.6**

**Fertility and Fertility Desires of the Sample Household**

**(1) Children Ever Born**

| | **No** | **Percent** |
|---|---|---|
| No child | 39 | 9.42 |
| One | 70 | 16.90 |
| Two | 157 | 37.92 |
| Three | 89 | 21.50 |
| Four | 34 | 8.22 |
| Five | 19 | 4.59 |
| Six | 4 | 0.97 |
| Seven | 1 | 0.24 |
| Eight | 1 | 0.24 |
| **Total** | **414** | **100** |

**(2) Male Children Ever Born**

| | **No** | **Percent** |
|---|---|---|
| No child | 82 | 19.81 |
| One | 178 | 43.00 |
| Two | 110 | 26.57 |
| Three | 36 | 8.70 |
| Four | 6 | 1.45 |
| Five | 2 | 0.48 |
| **Total** | **414** | **100** |

**(3) Female Children Ever Born**

| | No | Percent |
|---|---|---|
| No child | 159 | 38.41 |
| One | 161 | 38.89 |
| Two | 61 | 14.73 |
| Three | 24 | 5.80 |
| Four | 7 | 1.69 |
| Six | 1 | 0.24 |
| Eight | 1 | 0.24 |
| **Total** | **414** | **100** |

**(4) Desired Family Size (Persons)**

| | No | Percent |
|---|---|---|
| Three | 38 | 10.13 |
| Four | 224 | 59.73 |
| Five | 93 | 24.80 |
| Six | 16 | 4.27 |
| Seven | 4 | 1.07 |
| **Total** | **375** | **100** |

**(5) Children Survival**

| | No | Percent |
|---|---|---|
| No child | 39 | -- |
| One child | 73 | 19.47 |
| Two child | 155 | 41.33 |
| Three child | 90 | 24.00 |
| Four child | 34 | 9.07 |
| Five child | 18 | 5.00 |
| Six child | 3 | 0.80 |
| Seven child | 1 | 0.27 |
| Eight child | 1 | 0.27 |
| **Total** | **414** | **100** |

**TABLE – 4.7**

**Migration**

**(1) Residence**

| | No | Percent |
|---|---|---|
| Native | 309 | 72.9 |
| Migrant | 115 | 27.1 |

**(2) Reason for Migration**

| | Reasons | Percent |
|---|---|---|
| 1 | Non Production Agriculture | 2.98 |
| 2 | Family quarrel | 6.53 |
| 3 | Higher income | 28.72 |
| 4 | Higher Education | 16.96 |
| 5 | Encourage by | 1.64 |
| 6 | To start business | 15.18 |
| 7 | To improve economic status | 27.98 |

**(3) Migration with....**

| | | No | Percent |
|---|---|---|---|
| 1 | Alone | 31 | 26.96 |
| 2 | With family | 68 | 59.13 |
| 3 | With relative | 10 | 8.70 |
| 4 | With friends | 6 | 5.21 |
| | **Total** | **115** | |

**(4) Children Born**

| No. | Before Migration | Percent |
|---|---|---|
| 1 | 32 | 34.41 |
| 2 | 34 | 36.56 |
| 3 | 11 | 11.83 |
| 4 | 9 | 9.67 |
| 5 | 4 | 4.30 |
| 6 | 2 | 2.15 |
| 7 | 1 | 1.08 |
| | **93** | **100** |

**(5) After Migration**

| No. | After Migration | Percent |
|---|---|---|
| 1 | 36 | 31.85 |
| 2 | 38 | 33.62 |
| 3 | 15 | 13.27 |
| 4 | 11 | 9.73 |
| 5 | 6 | 5.31 |
| 6 | 5 | 4.42 |
| 7 | 1 | 0.90 |
| 8 | 1 | 0.90 |
| | **113** | **100** |

**(6) Residence Status**

| | No | Percent |
|---|---|---|
| Temporary | 32 | 27.83 |
| Permanent | 83 | 72.17 |

## TABLE – 4.8

### Family Planning

(1)

| | No. | Percent |
|---|---|---|
| Known | 391 | 92.2 |
| Believed | 390 | 92.0 |
| Accepted | 325 | 76.7 |

**(2) Reasons for not accepting**

| | Reasons | No. | Percent |
|---|---|---|---|
| (i) | Husband-wife do not want | 62 | 62.63 |
| (ii) | Non availability of contraception | 14 | 14.14 |
| (iii) | Difficulties in using contraceptives | 4.04 | 4.04 |
| (iv) | Social taboo | 9.09 | 9.09 |
| (v) | Any other | 10.10 | 10.10 |

**(3) Source of Knowledge**

| | Source | No. | Percent |
|---|---|---|---|
| (i) | Couple's parents | 5 | 1.54 |
| (ii) | Husband to wife | 18 | 5.54 |
| (iii) | Wife to husband | 2 | 0.61 |
| (iv) | Family doctor | 135 | 41.54 |
| (v) | Primary Health Clinic | 120 | 36.92 |
| (vi) | Health worker | 13 | 4.00 |
| (vii) | Media | 31 | 9.85 |
| (viii) | Others | 01 | -- |

**(4) Contraceptive methods**

| | No | Percent |
|---|---|---|
| Temporary | 126 | 38.77 |
| Permanent | 199 | 61.23 |
| **Total** | **325** | **100** |

**(5) Temporary methods**

| | No | Percent |
|---|---|---|
| Oral Pills | 28 | 22.22 |
| Coper T | 25 | 19.84 |
| Condom | 57 | 45.24 |
| Others | 16 | 12.70 |
| **Total** | **126** | **100** |

**(6) Sterilization**

| | No | Percentage |
|---|---|---|
| Males | 9 | 4.52 |
| Female | 190 | 95.48 |
| **Total** | **199** | **100** |

**(7) Sterilization Place**

| | No | Percent |
|---|---|---|
| Private | 124 | 62.31 |
| Public | 71 | 35.68 |
| Camp | 4 | 2.01 |

## TABLE – 4.9

### Health

**(1) Birth rate:-**

Last year's births

Males - 12

Females - 22

34

Birth rate = 16.35

**(2) Death rate:-**

Last year's deaths

Males - 4

Females - 5

9

Death rate = 4.33

**(3) Expenditure on Health:**

| Rs. | No. | Percent | Mean (Rs.) |
|---|---|---|---|
| 0-500 | 64 | 15.09 | |
| 501-1000 | 98 | 23.11 | |
| 1001-1500 | 67 | 15.80 | 1467 |
| 1501-2000 | 73 | 17.22 | |
| 2001-3000 | 72 | 17.00 | |
| 3001-4000 | 20 | 4.72 | |
| 4001-5000 | 14 | 3.30 | |
| 5001 | 16 | 3.76 | |
| Total | **424** | **100** | |

## TABLE – 4.10

### Immunization

(1)

| | Knowledge | Immunized | Kept record |
|---|---|---|---|
| No | 41<br>(9.7) | 62<br>(14.6) | 83<br>(19.5) |
| Yes | 383<br>(90.3) | 362<br>(85.4) | 341<br>(80.4) |

(2) **Immunization:**

| | BCG | Polio-1 | Polio-2 | Polio-3 |
|---|---|---|---|---|
| No | 173<br>(40.8) | 67<br>(15.8) | 67<br>(15.8) | 80<br>(18.9) |
| Yes | 25<br>(59.2) | 357<br>(84.2) | 357<br>(84.2) | 344<br>(81.1) |

(3)

| | Pulse Polio | DTP-1 | DTP-2 | DTP-3 |
|---|---|---|---|---|
| No | 142<br>(33.5) | 219<br>(51.7) | 280<br>(66.0) | 289<br>(68.2) |
| Yes | 282<br>(66.5) | 205<br>(48.3) | 144<br>(34.0) | 135<br>(31.8) |

(4)

| | Measles | Booster dose |
|---|---|---|
| No | 295<br>(69.6) | 296<br>(69.8) |
| Yes | 129<br>(30.4) | 128<br>(30.8) |

(5) **Immunized Place:**

| Comp | No. | Percent |
|---|---|---|
| O* | 45 | 10.6 |
| Private | 250 | 54.2 |
| Public | 127 | 30.0 |
| Comp | 22 | 9.2 |

* Service taken at home

## TABLE – 4.11

### Parental Preferences

**(1) Financial Burden (Children Education):**

| | | |
|---|---|---|
| N.A. | 66 | 15.6 |
| Very high burden | 48 | 11.3 |
| some what high burden | 67 | 15.8 |
| Family easy | 197 | 46.5 |
| D.K. | 46 | 10.8 |

**(2) Extra Facility (To improve education):**

| | | |
|---|---|---|
| N.A. | 261 | 61.6 |
| Vehicle | 51 | 12.6 |
| Separate study room | 55 | 13.0 |
| Study aid equipment | 20 | 4.7 |
| Others | 37 | 8.7 |

**(3) Extra Facility (Both Male and Female Children):**

| | | |
|---|---|---|
| Male child | 118 | 27.8 |
| Female child | 24 | 5.7 |
| Both | 13 | 3.1 |
| Non Both | 109 | 25.7 |
| None | 160 | 37.7 |

**(4) Parents' Choice for Children's Education:**

| Education | Sons | | Daughters | |
|---|---|---|---|---|
| | No. | Percent | No. | Percent |
| Primary | 3 | 0.7 | 9 | 2.1 |
| Higher Secondary | 14 | 3.3 | 31 | 7.3 |
| Graduation | 157 | 37.0 | 127 | 30.0 |
| P.G. (Science) | 18 | 4.2 | 16 | 3.8 |
| P.G. (Commerce) | 291 | 68.4 | 17 | 4.0 |
| B.E. | 36 | 8.5 | 21 | 5.0 |
| M.B.A. | 57 | 13.4 | 48 | 11.3 |
| Any other | 16 | 3.8 | 11 | 2.4 |
| Do not want | 94 | 22.2 | 144 | 34.0 |

**(5) Time Spared (Children's Education)**

| | | |
|---|---|---|
| N.A. | 142 | 33.5 |
| One hour | 77 | 18.2 |
| Two | 70 | 16.3 |
| Three | 26 | 6.1 |
| Can't spared | 109 | 25.5 |

**(6) Time Spared for Children by**

| | | |
|---|---|---|
| N.A. | 240 | 56.6 |
| Mother | 103 | 24.3 |
| Father | 23 | 5.4 |
| Grand Parents | 9 | 2.1 |
| Other Members | 10 | 2.4 |
| Both Parents | 33 | 7.7 |
| All family members | 4 | 1.4 |

**(7) Children's care taker (In absence of Parents):**

| | |
|---|---|
| N.A. | 391 |
| Grand parents | 16 |
| Baby sitting | 3 |
| Servant | 2 |
| Time adjustment | 13 |
| Neighbour | 9 |

# CHAPTER – V

# EMPIRICAL ANALYSIS OF MICRO DETERMINANTS OF POPULATION GROWTH

## 5.1 Introduction – Population Theories and Hypotheses

The study of the population theories indicates that these theories of various time-span differ a lot in its content and approach. The philosophers, thinkers and sociologists-economists propounded the various population theories based on the problems and prevailing circumstances of the societies concerned during the different time. In ancient theories of population – dating back to the time of Plato and Aristotle – over population was not considered a problem. On the contrary, population growth was considered to be a boon and not a bane. But it is also true that population growth was not very rapid in the old days due to high mortality rate and frequent wars between the states. This could be the reason why the ancient population theories were based on the hypothesis of high mortality and high fertility. Replacement of population could be major factor for maintaining the reasonable rate of population. The theories of Plato and Aristotle explain the theory of optimum population which was a basic need for the governance and security of the state. Machiavelli (1513) and Bodin (1576) asserted in their population theories that "large population was a source of strength". Thus ancient and medieval theories of population did not consider population growth as an obstacle in the socio-economic progress of the society but the strength of the state.

A remarkable change was observed in the theories of population with the emergence of Mercantilism in Europe. Population growth was now considered a necessity because of new inventions in the fields of science and technology and discoveries of new land areas. New inventions required more labour force for rapid production. Hence population growth was not a problem even in the mediaeval period of mercantilism. It was considered to be the strength of the state (Botero-1518). The naturalists also did not consider population growth a problem (Quesney-1759). But they did believe that development in the field of agriculture was more desirable than the development of industries. Grant's Mortality Bill (1662) based on the study of the population of London was a landmark in this field.

Malthus gave his first population theory in 1798 based on scientific attitude and backed by statistical data. His population theory was based on the hypothesis that "*Population is necessarily limited by the means of subsistence*". According to Malthus' theory, the product of food grains does not increase in the same proportion as the increase in population. According to him if this situation prevails, it will result in food scarcity and famine and then in the decrease in population. He strongly believed that natural forces, and not human endeavour, will control population growth.

Cannon (1861-1930) added two new concepts of population to the ancient concept of optimum population. He gave the optimum population theory based on the concepts of under population, optimum population and over population. According to his theory, population growth is not an obstacle if growth in total production is similar to population growth. According to his theory, the rate of population at maximum production is considered optimum population. After attaining this condition there is gradual decrease in production, and if the rate of population growth remains the same it is considered to be over population.

Spencer criticised Malthus' theory of population and gave biological theory of population with the belief that population growth will be controlled naturally. According to his theory, fertility is high when survival chances are low. This situation will create population pressure and production, and this in turn will result in advanced techniques of production. This will require the power to maintain life provided by better education, skills and control on self. In other words, the power to maintain life on the one hand and the power to propagate on the other hand, and he considered that the former varied directly and the later inversely with the development of the nervous system. Gini's theory of population (1930) is known as the cyclic theory of population. According to his theory, population tends to follow an evolution analogue to that of the life course of the individual passing through the successive stages of development, maturity and involution. Some population theories are based on the inverse relationship between diet and fertility. Doubleday (1841) and Castro (1952) in their population theories believed that rich and nutritive food intake results in the decrease of fertility.

At the end of the $19^{th}$ century and the initiation of the $20^{th}$ century sociological theories of population were propagated. These theories were based on the interrelationship of social advancement and revolution. Caste (1899) in his theory established a direct relationship between population growth and density. According to him population decreases with the increase is density of population. In Durkheim's (1893) view population growth generates social progress. Some theorists of this era were of the opinion that the rate of fertility decreases in the socially developed countries. Dupreel's (1928) theory of population is based on his observation that the size of family decreases during the process of urbanisation. According to Dumant's (1890) theory of social capillarity, the size of family is small in the societies where individuals strive to raise their social status.

Karl Marx tried to relate the growth of population with capitalism. According to him, with the progress of capitalism the problem of labour exploitation became grave. Karl Marx seriously thought over this problem and gave the Relative Surplus Population Theory. His theory explains how the present growth of population transforms into the problem of over population. He considers capitalism as responsible for the rise of this problem. Increase in unemployment is, according to him, the direct result of the progress of capitalism. The problem has been discussed in detail by Marx in his theory of Relative Surplus Population. It is also true that the development helps upgrade the standard of living. Not only this but the rate of child labour also decreases along with the decrease in birth rate as well as death rate. This means we cannot afford to have a biased opinion regarding capitalism. It is necessary to examine and analyse the rate of population growth in the various stages of the development of capitalism.

Blacker (1947), Thomson (1929), Notestein Borge (1945) and Cowgill (1949) explained the theory of population transition. Their theories of population indicate and explain the changes that take place in the quality and the rate of population alongwith economic development. According to their theories, it is in the third phase of population transition when the rate of population growth is low while the quality of population is high.

Easterline (1969), Becker (1960) and Leibenstein (1974) propounded the economic theories of fertility, which indicate the modern development in the thoughts on population growth. According to these thinkers parents take into consideration the economic condition of family before deciding to bring in a child in the family. The parents' decisions are based on their standard of living and cost benefit ratio. Easterline has tried to explain theory based on the fertility behaviour of individuals and their relative income. According to him, parents think of their children's future according to their own standard of living and wish that their children should be able to retain that standard of living.

Fertility decision is very important in the population theory of Becker, which he has explained with the help of economic analysis. Becker School presented micro economic model in which he explained how parental decision is important in deciding family size. The theory explains that demand and supply of children can be analogyzed with the demand for and supply of durable goods. Fertility and income are positively correlated. According to Becker's model parents' decisions are based on their speculations on their children's future. They are worried about their children's standard of living; hence, their decision for an additional child in the family depends upon this factor.

The economic factor is central in Leibenstein's population theory. According to him there is correlation between factors affecting population growth and the problems of economic development. Human welfare is central to economic development. Over population hinders economic development. In such condition, according to him, the rate of mortality decreases with increase in income, but fertility is not affected. This results in the increase in population.

These three theories have some common factors. These theories explain the reasons for the decrease in fertility. The theories also point out that the size of family depends upon the motivation of parents. With the increase in income other related factors help in deciding the family size. Leibenstein's population theory is based on cost and utility of children. The rate of utility obtained from children and the cost of raising children play a decisive role in deciding the number of children in a family. Leibenstein, Becker and Easterline's population theories are based on economic analysis. Their theories agree upon the hypothesis that with the increase in income the number of children in a family decreases.

## 5.2 Surat as Case Study

The basic unit for the micro analysis of the present study is family; hence, the problems and queries related to household are taken into consideration and analyzed to trace the pattern of population growth in Surat. An attempt has been made in this chapter to present the analysis of the primary data collected from 424 randomly selected households spread over the various electoral wards of Surat city.

## 5.3 Importance of Male-Children

Family is a social institution. Children are important both for parents and family since they provide certain social, cultural, economic and psychological satisfaction to the family in general and to parents in particular. Especially in traditional societies social values of children is more important for parents. But it is not possible to completely separate social value from economic value. According to Caldwell (1975, 1982, 1983), children are sources of both social and economic benefit. Both in traditional and modern societies the importance of male child in a family as heir to parental property is accepted. As in Confucian tradition male heirs are important to ensure the parents' welfare in the after life (Lee and Kim 1977; Williamson 1976), sons are important to perform important rituals in Hinduism and other formal religions (Wu, 1977).

Satisfactions from sons dominate in developing countries like India and preference for having the male child results in large family size. In Indian society, women are generally younger than their husbands and their life expectancy at adult ages is longer. On the other hand, their opportunities for employment and inheritance are less. Women normally require more economic support from their children than their husbands in their old ages. In the present study spousal age difference is 4.16 years (Chapter - IV), which is not very big, hence, it may not be of much relevance to the present study.

In many societies, male child is preferred over female child. There are many economic and sociological reasons. Male child is considered to provide security in old age. Male child fetches dowry in many communities. Besides, male child is considered necessary for performing funeral ceremony. The reasons for the preference for the male child vary.

The data from the Mysore Population Study (U.N., 1961) highlighted that more than 70 per cent of the women respondents had expected to rely on their children for old age security. Ramu (1988) in Kolar Gold Field in Karnataka, South Indian observed that sons have been considered as a source of security and protection in one's old age. Population studies conducted outside India also indicate that sons are considered valuable both economically and socially. Findings from the studies conducted in Taiwan (Mueller, 1972) and Thailand (Arnold and Pejarananda, 1977) have reported that parents who ever perceived greater economic utility and old age security from children opted for larger family size. A study conducted in Kerala (Jayasree, 1989) indicates that the respondents who expected economic support and inheritance of family property from sons lead to higher fertility (3.1 and 3.1 respectively) than those who did not expect such support (2.7 and 2.9). Another study in Tamil Nadu (Devraj, 1991) also indicates that the social values, continuation of family name and tradition and performing rituals and funeral rites – have shown a significant effect on children ever born.

## 5.4 Total Children and Female Children in Family

Preference for the male child can be examined through the relationship between total family size and proportion of female children in family. One would expect a positive relationship between proportion of female children and family size in the presence of the preference for male child.

### *Empirical Results*

The results of the present study indicate that:

(1) In larger families where total number of children is more, the number of female children is more than male children.

(2) In the families having single child 81.9 percent families have male children.

(3) In 51.75 per cent families have more daughters than sons. 72.5 per cent of these families have one son and two daughters each.

(4) In the families with five children 42.9 percent families have more than fifty per cent girl children in the family.

From the statistical analysis shown in table - 5.1, the result show association between the total number of children in a family and number of female children in a family and the result is statistically significant. It shows a wide difference between observed values and expected values.

### 5.5 Ideal Family Sizes and Female Child in Family

There is a difference between the ideal family size and the total number of children in a family. It is quite obvious that parents with less number of children desire a small family but it has been observed that sometimes families with large number of children are also desirous of keeping the size of their family smaller because in such cases, one of the reason for the large number of children could be their preference for a male child in the family. The size of family is likely to be smaller where parents want only one male child, but in other total number of children is more. In the families where the number of female children is more, the size of family is comparatively larger, but the fact is, in such cases, parents actually desire a small family. This is observed in table - 5.2.

The analysis shows that there is statistically significant proportion of female children in a family and ideal family size.

(1) The parents in 46.66 per cent families where more than 50 per cent children are females believe that the ideal family size should be four.

(2) According to 33.3 per cent households without a female child in the family believe that 4 is the ideal family size.

In the households where the number of children – even female children – is more, they also accept that the size of family should be small.

### 5.6 Economic Status of a Household and Family Size

Economic status of a household is a major factor which affects the total number of children of a household, both directly and indirectly. Higher income is generally associated with better occupation, which needs higher education and training, and these in turn help reducing the family size. Freedman (1959) gives some explanations for the conventional inverse relationship between income and family size. According to him, higher income groups have fewer children.

Freedman's explanations are as follows:

(1) High expenditure on child rearing is an economic burden.

(2) Most people of high income group living in cities desire less children.

(3) Such people neither desire to increase family size nor do they have any other economic value for children, except providing them higher education.

(4) High-income families not only spend large amounts on children, but also spend money to hire labour because they do not see their children as prospective labour force. Caldwell (1982) also opines that because parents do not see their children as prospective labour, their expectations from their children are very high. Hence, they spend more on child rearing. As a result, they want less number of children in the family.

Numerous studies on the relationship between economic status and family size conducted so far yield different results. Some of the studies have shown negative relationship between the two; while the findings of some studies indicate positive relationship and some of the results find no relationship between economic status and family size. The reasons for the difference in results are that apart from income, other factors also play a decisive role on family size. Micro and Macro studies also show different trends. Generally it is believed that economic standards and availability or non-availability of family planning devices play an important role in deciding family size.

The results of a study conducted by Freedman and Slesinger (1961) show that there is no negative relationship between income and fertility in the non-farm couples but in the farming migrants there was a substantial inverse association between income and fertility. The results of a study conducted in Iran by Paydarfer and Sarram (1970) indicate an inverse relationship between income and fertility. Bernhardt (1972) in Sweden also observed that the average number of births was higher among the lower income families. The negative association between economic status and fertility has also been noticed in India. Poti and Dutt (1960) in their study on West Bengal observed that the average number of children born to the higher income families was less (2.34) than in the lower income families (2.55). A study conducted by Anand (1966) in Chandigarh also indicates inverse relationship between fertility and economic prosperity. A fertility survey conducted in Lucknow (Hussain, 1970) also shows inverse relationship between marital fertility rate and household income. Similarly, the Greater Bombay Fertility and Planning Survey (Rele, Kanitkar, 1980) also shows the similar trend.

Some studies conducted in India do not show any definite relationship between income and fertility. In his Central India Study Driver (1973) derived that the level of fertility was higher both in low-income groups and high-income groups. Similarly the studies of Majmudar (1960) in Kanpur and Mukherjee and Singh (1961) in Lucknow did not find a definite relationship between income and fertility.

## 5.7 Total Children and Income of Household

Some studies indicate that the relationship between income and family size varies at both micro and macro levels. The results of some of the studies do not indicate any consistent pattern between family size and economic status.

The present study on Surat does not find any significant association between the two variables. The results show a mixed trend. The detailed analysis of table 5.3 show the following results:

(i) 43.2 per cent households with Rs.1 lakh and more income per annum have only two children.

(ii) 29.6 per cent of families having Rs.25,000 or less income per annum have three children.

(iii) 39.5 per cent households earning between Rs.50,000 and 1 lakh per annum have two children.

(iv) 51.6 per cent of households with three children earn between Rs.50,000 and 1 lakh.

(v) 3.7 per cent households with five children earn Rs. 25,000 or less per annum.

These statistics clearly show that there is no clear pattern related to income and number of children.

The reasons for such varied results could be as follows:

(i) This is a micro level study based on small sample size.

(ii) The area of the study is urban where no definite relationship has been observed between good occupation and higher income.

(iii) Members of household are not necessarily educated.

As indicated in table - 5.3, chi-square significance value is more than 5 per cent, it therefore, means, there is no statistically significant relationship between these two variables. There is weak or no association between income of the household and total number of children in the family.

### 5.8 Total Children and Occupational Status of the Household

The relationship between the total number of children in the family and the economic status of the household has been examined through statistical analysis. The family status is further categorised as general, industrial, non-industrial (service-class household) and mixed (with family members either engaged both in occupations and services). The highest number of children in a family is six. The analysis of table - 5.4 gives the follows results:

(i) The proportion of service class households having two or three children is 61 per cent.

(ii) The proportion of industrial households having two or three children is 53.3 per cent.

(iii) The proportion of mixed status households having two or three children is 66.7 per cent.

Thus, the proportion of service class households with two or three children is the highest. Second comes mixed households and the last is the industrial households.

In this case, the null hypothesis is that there is no association between the occupational status of a household and the total number of children. However, as indicated in table - 5.4, as per chi-square, significance value is lower than 1 per cent level. Therefore, the null hypothesis is rejected and it means that there is a strong relationship between occupational status of a family and number of children. It can be argued that the number of children is less in service class people. In other words, service class people tend to have smaller family size.

### 5.9 Family Type and Income Group in Household

Family type is divided into two groups: joint family type and single/nuclear family for the purpose of this study. On the other hand, households are divided according to various income groups. An attempt has been made to find whether these two variables are associated (Table - 5.5).

The study reveals the following:

(i) The proportion of households with low income living in joint families is less than the proportion of households with high income living in joint families.

As indicated in table - 5.5, in the households having income above one lakh per annum, 55.7 per cent live in joint families while only 29.6 per cent households having annual income Rs.25000 or less live in joint families.

(ii) The proportion of joint family is more in the high-income groups.

Table - 5.5 indicates family types and household groups according to the level of income. It has been tried to find out the family status according to income. The results indicate that 71.5 per cent of household in the joint family category earn Rs.50,000 and more annually.

According to Pearson chi-square the significance value is 0.00126. It implies that the two variables are strongly related.

### 5.10 Family Type and Occupational Status of the Family

A household is recognized by its type and occupational status. These give an idea of both the total members in the family and earning member in the family. Family type and occupational status of a household are correlated.

It has been observed that most of the members living in single/nuclear families are earning members. As both husband and wife are engaged in services, they have to work more and spare more time for economic activities. These factors control the number of children in such families. Joint families reveal an altogether different scenario. Majority households living in joint families are engaged in mixed occupational category, i.e. some of the members are engaged in occupations while some others are engaged in services. Such families have more earning members and family responsibilities are divided. Hence, the parents do not have direct responsibility of bringing up children. This is one of the main reasons why joint families have larger number of children.

The analysis of table - 5.6 confirms the above observations:

(1) 52.3 per cent household in mixed occupational category live in joint families.

(2) There are 68.6 per cent households living in single/nuclear families having non-industrial occupational status.

The statistical analysis of table - 5.6 exhibits a high $x^2$ and this value is highly significant, hence, both the variables are highly associated.

### 5.11 Ideal Family Size and Income Groups of the Household

The ideal number of total children in association with income in each household of the sample population is shown in table - 5.7. Earlier, the relationship between the number of children and the level of income was not confirmed. As far as ideal family size is concerned, opinions expressed by the sample population were independent of their income group. The statistics presented in table - 5.7 indicate that majority of the respondents in Surat are of the opinion that four is the ideal family size, irrespective of their economic status. 29.6 per cent households with Rs. 25000 income per annum, 29.6 per cent households with income between Rs.25,000 and 50,000, 44.3 per cent in the income group above Rs.1 lakh believe that the ideal family size should be 4 persons. Thus, in the higher income groups, more households preferred for four persons as an ideal family. Since significance of the chi-square value is .07874, it implies that ideal family size is independent of income. The view on ideal family size is uniform and does not depend on the level of income.

### 5.12 Ideal Family Size and Occupational Status of the Family

It is not possible to decide the occupational status of a family from the income of the family. But it can be discerned as to what should be the ideal family size as per occupational status of the family from the opinions given by the sample population. The analysis of table - 5.8 shows a wide difference between observed value and expected value. 73.3 per cent of the households in industrial category believe that four members is the ideal family size, 32.6 per cent household in service class and 13.0 per cent household in the mixed occupational category consider four person family as the ideal family.

### 5.13 Educational Level of Household and Family Size

Educational level of the household has been widely used by the researchers as one of the important determinant of family size of the household. Educational level of the household affects – both directly and indirectly – fertility by forming the psychological orientation favouring small family size, and also by indirectly influencing the other social, economic and demographic factors associated with fertility.

It has been observed that in the households where the level of education is high, the level of female education also increases considerably. In the present study, the level of education up to high school and above is 80.13 per cent (Chapter - IV), while in 52.21 per cent (Chapter - IV) households females have obtained higher education. It has been observed that women's fertility is considerably affected in the households where the level of education in women is found high.

The results of several researchers indicate that the number of total children and number of male children decreases in the households with higher education. This effect is particularly observed where female education is high. It is quite possible that either the level of education in women and fertility are highly associated or partly associated.

Higher education and employment opportunities for women in cities upgrade the status of women in society. Family responsibilities are equally shared and borne by family members. Women are more free to take their own decisions regarding the number of children in family. Thus in the families where women attain higher education the number of children is less (Mandelbaum 1974, Dixon 1976, Stycos 1978).

Empirical research evidence over the last thirty years indicates that the effect of education – particularly women's education – in often observed to be negative on fertility in India as well as in the world (Jaff 1959, U.N. 1961, Mincer 1962, Thompson and Lewis 1965, Caldwell 1978, Mitchell 1972, Jain 1981, Jain and Nag 1986, Sathar and Kazi 1988, Srikanthan and Bhate 1989). All these researches indicate that in the families with high education the number of children is less.

According to the World Fertility Survey (1964), differences in fertility due to education are very large. Fertility decreases with increased educational level. The differences in total fertility rates between the least and the most educated women were highest in Latin American countries, amounting to about 4 to 5 children. In Africa and Asian countries it is 1 to 2 children. U.S. Commission on Population Growth and the American Future (1972) noted that higher educational attainment was closely associated with smaller families. In less educated women the rate of fertility is found to be higher.

On the basis of the studies conducted in England, Wales, the Netherlands, Norvey and West Germany, Cochrane (1979, 1983) observed that there is an inverse relationship between fertility and education. In a review of studies conducted in Sichuan, China, Freedman (1988) observed that the fertility has remarkably declined gradually from 1967-1970 to 1979-1982 at every increasing educational level both in rural and urban sectors.

Several studies conducted in India also indicate inverse relationship between education and fertility. Driver (1963) in his study conducted in Central India observed that for the women without any formal education, the number of children is larger (average 5-0 per women) than those with high school or college education (3.9 per women). A study conducted in Mumbai in 1989 (Bhargav and Saxena) reveals that women with education below S.S.C. gave birth to an average of 2.9 children as against 2.1 children for those with higher education. The recent studies conducted in the urban areas indicate that factors other than education also affect fertility; hence, the gap in the number of children in the educated women and uneducated or less educated women is not very big.

Some of the studies conducted in the developed countries do not indicate inverse relationship between education and fertility. Factors other than education are also responsible for less number of children (Mason et.al., 1971, Wolfe, 1980). A study conducted in the United States by Sutton and Wunderlich (1967) did not find any association between education and number of children in the family. The results derived from the surveys conducted both in the developed and developing countries indicate that in any area or country the association between education and fertility is not very strong.

### 5.14 Total number of Children and Education (Years of Schooling)

The present study attempts to analyse the effect of education on fertility decision. The results derived from the sample study indicate that the level of education is high in Surat, especially in women. The results also indicate that high education in women affects the fertility of mothers. Even in children's education, both the proportion of education and expenditure on education show an increasing trend. There is no association between the level of education of the head of the family and the number of children, because as per social and economic norms parents prefer two or three children in the family irrespective of the education of parents. They also want to provide good education to their children.

The following two observations have been derived from the study:

(i) The educational level of the head of the household does not affect the number of children.

(ii) With the increase of education in the family, the education in women also increases.

The analysis of table - 5.9 indicates that the significance value of relationship between fertility and education years of schooling (highest) is less than one percent, therefore, the null hypothesis that there is no association between the number of children and education is rejected. The family size and household education (highest) are strongly related.

(i) In urban area 62.0 per cent families with high educational status and 60.5 per cent families with low educational status have either two or three children, irrespective of their level of education. Thus 61.3 per cent of the total families in Surat have two or three children.

(ii) In 60.6 per cent of families with two children the level of education is up to higher secondary and above.

(iii) The level of education in 56.8 per cent families having five children is up to high school. This is higher than those families with higher education (43.2).

Thus, the findings show inverse relationship between the level of education of households and number of children and this relationship is statistically significant.

### 5.15 Total Children and Annual Expenses on Education per Child

The analysis of table - 5.10 yields the following results:

The average expenditure on children's education affects the quality of education in a family. Families having three children do not find this expenditure as an additional burden, but in the families having more than three children the expenses on children's education is an extra burden, hence, the parents are unable to provide higher education to their children, (a) 95.2 per cent of families spending Rs. 1000 to Rs. 2000 per child annually on education do not have more than three children. (b) 95.2 per cent of families spending between Rs. 3000 and 5000 per annum per child on education do not have more than three children.

The total number of children in a family and average annual expenditure per child are negatively correlated and this relationship is statistically significant because significance value of chi-square is less than one. It exhibits a wide difference between observed values and expected values.

## 5.16 Ideal Family Size and Years of Schooling in the Household

Total number of persons in a household is taken into consideration in deciding the ideal family size. The study of table - 5.11 indicates that families with high educational level opt for small family size.

(i) Out of the total families, 99.2 per cent families with education up to high school level consider five persons in a family as ideal family size,

(ii) 98 per cent families out of the total families with higher secondary level education also believe that maximum five persons in a family is the ideal family size.

(iii) 95.8 per cent families out of the total number of families having college and higher education also prefer for a five persons family as the ideal family size.

(iv) Out of the total families 17.9 per cent families with education upto high school, level and 43.3 per cent families with higher education consider four members in a family as ideal family size.

The results of the analyses indicate that the ideal number of family members is limited to maximum of five in the educated families. The relationship between households' preference for number of children and education is negative and it is statistically significant. As the level of education goes up, the preference for large family size declines.

### 5.17 Family Size and Religion

Religion is considered one of the important determinants of family size. The effects of religion on population growth are more evident in the developing countries, mainly in the rural areas and at the initial phase of urbanization. The status of women, up to a certain extent, varies according to the religious beliefs and value to which they belong. e.g. Catholic Christianity do not permit family planning. This naturally affects fertility of women. But in India, as it has been generally observed, Christian women enjoy a slightly better status than their Hindu or Muslim counterparts. The same is true in case of Parsi women, especially in Gujarat and Surat.

Studies conducted in various countries indicate that the fertility in women differs in different religious groups. Some notable studies are conducted by Sinha (1957) in India, Yauken (1969) in Lebanon, Rizk (1963) in Egupt, Kirk (1969) in Malaysia and Matras (1973) in Israel. A study conducted by Tuladhar (1989) in Nepal revealed that the TMFR (6.86) was higher in non-Hindus than in the Hindus (6.73).

Several studies in India conducted by scholars brought out the fertility differentials in various religious group across the country. Some of the noteworthy studies are by Driver (1963), U.N. (1961), Saxena (1973), R.G. India (1976 and 1980), Srinivasan and associates (1977), Rele and Kanitkar (1980) and Zachariah (1984). Results of Fertility survey conducted by R.G. India (1980) indicate that the TFR was higher among the Muslims both in rural and urban areas (5.03 and 3.94 respectively), followed by the Hindus (4.46 and 3.09 respectively). TFR was found to be the lowest among the Christians (3.50 and 2.09 respectively).

***Total Children in the Family and Religion***

The present micro level study reveals that average numbers of children among Muslims were found to be 3.89 and this is higher compared to average number of children among Hindu women. The Hindu women have 2.35 children. But the differences in number of children between Hindu and Muslim women are not statistically significant (Table - 5.12). It, therefore, means that religions factor does not play important role in explaining variation in family size.

**5.18 Ideal Family Size and Religion**

The analysis of table - 5.13 shows the norms of ideal family size as per the religion of the households. The total number of family members is found more in Muslim households than in the Hindu households. Apart from religious belief other factors like family type, education in women, women employment, level of education in children, marriage system etc. also play a vital role in deciding the ideal family size.

Table - 5.13 yields following results:

(i) Only 6.9 per cent Hindu households desire five persons in a family, while in Muslims 27.3 per cent households accept five persons as ideal family size.

(ii) In an average Muslim household ideal family size is found to be 4.57 persons, which is higher than that of average Hindu households (4.18).

(iii) 82.8 per cent Hindu households have four members in the family, while only 10.4 per cent Muslim households have 4 persons in the family.

The analysis indicates high chi-square value and (table - 5.13) the significant value to be zero. This shows that the ideal family size according to the respondents belief and their religions are highly co-related.

**Family Size and Religion**

(1) Family size and religion do not have statistically significant relationship.

(2) Belief of family size and religion are strongly related. Relationship is statistically significant.

(3) Belief is not translated in action.

(4) Economic forces dominate other factors including religious belief in determining family size.

**5.19 Population Growth and Migration**

Fertility, mortality and migration are the three principal components of the population study. Internal migration of population does not affect population growth but it affects the distribution of population. It is important to study the trends of migration to understand the process of urbanization, as internal migration is residential mobility from one place to another within the same country. From the various types of internal mobility the study of inter-state migration and migration from rural to urban sectors is very important because these two largely affect the socio-economic development of the region.

Migrants are usually compared with all non-migrants (Bouge, 1951), the comparison is also with time span and migrant population. In the present study, migrants living in Surat for more than twenty-five years are taken as non-migrants. Several studies have been conducted on migrant population with various objectives. Some of the important objectives of such studies are as follows:

(i) To find out the reasons for migration.

(ii) To study the problems arising from migration and to assimilate and find solutions to these problems.

(iii) To form theories of migration based on the findings of the results or the studies on migrants in various places.

Many of the studies available on migration are based on secondary information available. Some of these are based on the comparisons of time and place.

Age of the migrants at the time of migration and their sex are the two very important variables in the study of the migration of population. As Kuroda (1967) points outs "*without much doubt the most universally valid of all migration differentials is the age differential and there are few exceptions to the rule that migration is selective of persons in young adults' working ages.*" Generally, the age of the migrants is found to be between 15-20 and 30-35 years. In a study conducted in the Soviet Union (Daragan, 1967) the age of migrants was found between 20 and 29 years, while in studies conducted in Germany and Hungary (Thirring, 1962, 1967) on the internal migration the age of the migrants was 20 to 24 and 18 to 20 years. According to census record in Japan in 1960 the age of migrants was between 15 and 29 years. (Ueda, 1967). The age of 43 per cent of migrants in Mumbai during the years 1951-61 was recorded to be between 20 and 35 years (Zachariah, 1966).

The average age of the migrants is between 15 and 30 years. The age of migrants is very important in deciding the objectives for migration. It has been observed that migration at the above mentioned age takes place mainly for two reasons: either to earn money or to pursue higher studies. It has also been observed that generally such migrants prefer to live in joint families in the initial years of their migration and there after they get married and settle their own separate families. If the migrant individual is already married, he comes to the city alone and there after he brings his family. Thus, a migrant individual prepares himself to accept the additional socio-economic burdens. This also affects the socio-economic development of the urban area. The married couples plan their family after migration; hence, children are born after migration. This affects the natural population growth of the urban area.

Both males and females migrate from one place to another but it has been observed that number of migratory women is found to be large only in short distance migration (Ravenstein, 1885-1889, Lee, 1966). Generally, men initiate the process of migration and settle socially and economically at the new place, while women migrate after men are well established and posses a secure place in the new society. Contrary to this general trend of male migration, in the countries of Latin America, Europe, North America etc. when the heavy industries were started it was the women folk who had initiated the process of migration (UN, 1957). In Soviet Union (Daragon, 1967), the number of female migrants was less while in a study conducted in Canada (George, 1970) the number of both male and female migrant between 1901 and 1961 was almost equal.

In the metro cities of India – Mumbai, Chennai, Delhi and Kolkata – the number of male migrants was quite large between 1941-51 (Bouge and Zachariah, 1970) the number of male migrants was the highest in Mumbai. The principal reason of this sex-selective migration was found to be the social-cultural position of women in the cultural environment of Indian social life.

Education is another important reason for migration. The number of male migrant is quite large than female migrants for educational purpose. The level of education among migrants decide their socio-economic status. The importance of education is decided by human capital and genetic differences of the migrants. But it is also equally true that the educational status is found to be comparatively higher than others in the places from where they migrate. The level of education was found to be lower in migrants than the natives of the Mexico district in the census conducted in 1960 (Browning, 1967). In a study conducted in Ghana (Caldwell, 1968) it has been derived that there is relationship between the period of schooling in migrants and propensity to migrate from rural area to urban area. One of the main reasons for migration in U.K. and Canada was also education. In a study conducted in Canada (Stone, 1969) the level of education among the migrants of the age group between 25 and 39 years was found to be higher than the natives. The level of education in migrants is mainly decided by the quality of labour force required in the urban area. The urban places where qualified labour force is required the level of education among the labour force is found to be higher.

The results of the present study do not vary much from the results available of the previous studies conducted so far. The results of this micro level study indicate that the main reasons for migration for the individuals between age 15 and 35 years are better job opportunities available in Surat and higher income. The number of male migrants is more than female migrants. Initially they prefer joint family system. Married migrants have given birth to less number of children after their migration.

### 5.20 Total Number of Children and Migration

The previous hypothesis that total number of children in migrant families is larger than in the native urban families is not strongly substantiated. These two variables are not strongly related because according to chi-square analysis the $x^2$ value is 5.14857 and not significant (Table - 5.14). The reasons for the above stated results are: (i) The migrants who have been living in Surat for more than 10 years have adjusted themselves in the socio-economic set up of the city, hence they prefer less children. (ii) If they are married after migration they want to concentrate on the better upbringing and education of their children than on the number of children. In other words, they prefer quality of children to quantity of children.

In the native urban households, the average number of children is 2.21 while the average number of children in the migrant households is 2.09. The average number of children in the migrant households was 2.24 while the average number of children in the migrant households after migrating to Surat is 2.16, which is less than the previous average.

### 5.21 Ideal Family Size and Migration

Migrant households are found to be conscious regarding the size of their families. In their opinion and belief regarding the ideal family size they do not differ from their urban native counterparts for the simple reason that they have to bear all the socio-economic responsibilities of their families. Hence they also prefer less number of members in the household. In their opinion regarding ideal family size the urban natives opt for 4.02 average number of persons in a family while the migrants opt for 4.11 members in an ideal family. The opinion of the migrants regarding the average number of family member is a little higher than the natives because they already had children before they came to Surat. No association is found between migrants and their opinion regarding ideal family size because according to chi-square analysis the significant value of these two variables is more than five per cent (Table - 5.15).

### 5.22 Family Type and Migration

Migrants have shifted and settled in Surat at a comparatively younger age. The number of male migrants is larger than female migrants. Initially they prefer to live in joint family; hence, the total years of their migration play an important role in deciding the relationship between family type and migration. 48.5 per cent of urban natives live in joint families while 55.7 per cent (Table - 5.16) of migrants live in joint families 18.3 per cent of migrants live in single families but they have separated after acquiring social and economical stability. 26.1 per cent households started living in single families soon after marriage.

As indicated in table - 5.16 the significant value of chi-square is high and significant (0.00189), which is lower than one per cent. Hence migration and type of family indicate interrelationship and they are highly associated to each other.

Whether total number of children in a family help to decide the opinion of the individuals regarding ideal family size has been studied in tables - 5.19 and 5.20. The opinion regarding ideal family size and the type of family has also been analysed in table - 5.21.

### 5.23 Total Number of Children and Ideal Family Size

People believe that the total number of members is an ideal family should be four irrespective of the number of children in their own families. 91 per cent of households having four children in the family opine for four members in an ideal family (parents + 2 children). Total number of children in a family and ideal family size are highly associated because the analysis finds out that the $x^2$ value is high and significant (Table - 5.17). This opinion seems to be quite obvious because naturally the families with less number of children opt for a small family while the families having more number of children change their opinion when they find economic burden of more children in the family.

### 5.24 Total Number of Children and Family Type

It has been observed from the study of the relationship between total number of children and family type (Table - 5.18) that households having large number of children live in joint families 66.7 per cent of households having four children live in joint families, while 60.9 per cent households having 5 and more children live in joint families. However, 58.4 per cent households having only one child live in single/nuclear families.

According to Pearson's chi-square, value is 21.18292 and highly significant (Table - 5.18). Total number of children and family type are strongly correlated. Thus, type of family plays dominant role in determining family size. The cost of rearing children in nuclear family is very high and therefore couples in nuclear family prefer to have smaller family size.

### 5.25 Ideal Family Size and Family Type

People living in joint families opt for higher number of members in a family because they are aware of the advantages of joint family system. But these advantages are immediate or short-term advantages. They become aware of the disadvantages of joint family system later on. They become aware of the economic stability of their individual family, their children's education and their future prospects after they spend a long time in a joint family. The members of joint family system are found to possess mixed occupational status, i.e. some are engaged in occupations or services and some are engaged in manufacturing units. Most members of the families are earning even if the level of total household income in low.

Only 21.7 and 22.4 per cent households from joint families believed that the total number of members in a household should be 3 and 4 respectively, while others having this opinion regarding ideal family size lived in single/nuclear families. As per chi-square analysis (Table - 5.19), it has been concluded that the ideal family size and family type are highly associated because significant value is zero.

### 5.26 Housing Condition

The ownership of house, its construction type, availability of clean air, quality of drinking water available to the habitants and the number of people occupying the habitat are the factors to be considered while deciding the housing condition. Housing condition is also greatly affected by the income of the occupants. These factors have been analyzed in Table - 5.20.

Ownership of house and the type of ownership, average members in a household, separate kitchen and sanitation, etc. has already been discussed in Chapter - IV. The analysis of Table - 5.20 in this chapter indicates that previous hypothesis that people with high income possess their own houses has been proven wrong. The analysis shows that income and ownership of house has no relationship because 87.6 per cent of total households have their own houses.

Of course, each one of the sample population has opined for own house. Especially those who belong to service class or mixed occupational category insist that they must possess their own houses for the simple reason that both government and non-government monetary help is easily available at very suitable conditions. Rates of interest are also gradually decreasing plus the interest on housing loan in exempted from income tax. Because of the above stated reasons it is not necessary that only people with high income can possess their own houses. Significant value of these two variables is more than one per cent (Table - 5.20), therefore the hypothesis that income and ownership of house has no relationship proves true.

### 5.27 Summary

The chapter begins with a summary description of population theories, especially those theories which are based on the hypotheses regarding population growth. Various population theories attempt to explain reasons for population growth, both at local and national levels. These theories have been included in this chapter as part of review of existing literature based on population theories. Some of the common hypotheses are found to be proven according to population theories. Some of the hypotheses of the related population theories are given below:

(i) High mortality, high fertility.

(ii) Replacement of population is the main cause of high fertility.

(iii) Population is necessarily limited by the means of subsistence.

(iv) The concepts of under, over and optimum population are closely interrelated.

(v) Fertility is high when survival chances of children are low.

(vi) Personal achievement, development, maturity, involution are important in deciding family size.

(vii) Social development and urbanization are also important in deciding family size.

(viii) The relative surplus population is next to over population.

(ix) Fertility and income factor are inversely related.

(x) The number of children in a family depends upon the standard of living of parents.

(xi) The number of children in a family also depends upon parents' concern over the future living standard of their children.

(xii) The number of children in a family depends upon the parents' socio economic attitude for the children.

The chapter also attempts to provide explanation on the factors deciding the number of children in a family. These decisive factors are income, religion, education, occupational status of the household, population migration and parents' attitude towards children. Some contradictory results are also found in the analyses of some of the researchers. Some researchers indicate that the number of children in a household is less when income of a family is more, while results of some of the researches indicate no correlation between income and fertility.

The results derived from primary information are analyzed and presented in this chapter. These results mainly indicate the various factors like occupational status, education, religion, family type, parents' preference for children etc., which affect the number of children in a family. This has been shown through cross table analyses by finding relationship between any two variables indicated above. The following are the results derived from the analyses of tables:

(i) In the households having large number of children, the number of girl children is more.

(ii) The households having large number of female children also believe that the size of family should be small.

(iii) There is no relationship between total number of children in a family and the total income of a family.

(iv) Occupational status of a household affects the number of children in a family.

(v) The total income of the households is high in joint families. Majority of joint families possess mixed occupational status.

(vi) Educational expenses on children play a decisive role in deciding the number of children in a family.

(vii) The number of children is less in the families having higher education.

(viii) Religion does not affect the number of children.

(ix) Fertility rate in migrant population has decreased after their migration.

(x) No difference has been found in the number of children in migrant families and urban native families.

(xi) Family type is important in deciding number of children in a family.

(xii) In their initial stage of migration, people prefer to live in joint families.

**TABLE – 5.1**

**Total Children and Female Children (Proportion)**

| Total Children<br>Count<br>Exp. Val. | Female Children in the Family | | | Row Total |
|---|---|---|---|---|
| | Nil | ≤ 50% | Above 50% | |
| One | 59<br>30.9 | 0<br>27.1 | 13<br>13.9 | 72 |
| Two | 60<br>70.9 | 92<br>62.1 | 13<br>31.9 | 165 |
| Three | 30<br>40.8 | 32<br>35.8 | 33<br>18.4 | 95 |
| Four | 7<br>10.3 | 12<br>9.0 | 5<br>4.6 | 24 |
| Five | 6<br>9.0 | 6<br>7.9 | 9<br>4.1 | 21 |
| Column Total | 162 | 142 | 73 | 377 |

| Chi-Square | Value | DF | Significance |
|---|---|---|---|
| Pearson | 104.27273 | 8 | 0.00000 |
| Pearson's R | 0.29111 | | |

**TABLE – 5.2**

**Ideal Family Size and Female Children (Proportion)**

| Person Count Exp. Val. | Female Children in the Family | | | Row Total |
|---|---|---|---|---|
| | Nil | ≤ 50% | Above 50% | |
| Nil | 85<br>82.9 | 80<br>72.7 | 28<br>37.4 | 193 |
| Three | 11<br>7.3 | 1<br>6.4 | 5<br>3.3 | 17 |
| Four | 54<br>52.0 | 46<br>45.6 | 21<br>23.4 | 121 |
| Five | 9<br>15.0 | 13<br>13.2 | 13<br>6.8 | 35 |
| Six | 3<br>4.7 | 2<br>4.1 | 6<br>2.1 | 11 |
| Column Total | 162 | 142 | 73 | 377 |

| **Chi-Square** | **Value** | **DF** | **Significance** |
|---|---|---|---|
| Pearson | 27.69648 | 8 | 0.00054 |
| Pearson's R | 0.11592 | | |

**TABLE – 5.3**

**Total Children and Family Income (Annual)**

| Total Children Count Exp. Val. | Income in Groups (Rs.) | | | | Row Total |
|---|---|---|---|---|---|
| | ≤ 25000 | 25001-50000 | 50001-1 lakh | Above one lakh | |
| Nil | 7<br>2.8 | 10<br>11.8 | 17<br>19.5 | 9<br>9.0 | 43 |
| One | 3<br>4.6 | 20<br>19.7 | 29<br>32.6 | 20<br>15.1 | 72 |
| Two | 6<br>10.5 | 45<br>44.9 | 75<br>74.2 | 38<br>34.4 | 164 |
| Three | 8<br>6.1 | 25<br>26.0 | 49<br>43.0 | 13<br>19.9 | 95 |
| Four | 2<br>1.5 | 8<br>6.6 | 11<br>10.9 | 3<br>5.0 | 24 |
| Five | 1<br>1.4 | 7<br>6.0 | 9<br>10.0 | 5<br>4.6 | 22 |
| Column Total | 27 | 115 | 190 | 88 | 420 |

| **Chi-Square** | **Value** | **DF** | **Significance** |
|---|---|---|---|
| Pearson | 22.51338 | 15 | 0.28853 |
| Pearson's R | -0.01345 | | |

**TABLE – 5.4**

**Total Children and Occupation Status**

| Total Children Count Exp. Val. | Occupation Status of the Family | | | | Row Total |
|---|---|---|---|---|---|
| | Ordinary | Industrial | Non-Industrial | Mixed | |
| Nil | 8<br>8.1 | 10<br>4.8 | 14<br>15.0 | 13<br>17.2 | 45 |
| One | 21<br>12.9 | 7<br>7.6 | 23<br>23.9 | 21<br>27.5 | 72 |
| Two | 26<br>29.6 | 20<br>17.5 | 44<br>54.9 | 75<br>63.0 | 165 |
| Three | 16<br>17.0 | 4<br>10.1 | 42<br>31.6 | 33<br>36.5 | 95 |
| Four | 3<br>4.3 | 2<br>2.5 | 7<br>8.0 | 12<br>9.2 | 24 |
| Five | 2<br>4.1 | 2<br>2.4 | 11<br>7.6 | 8<br>8.8 | 23 |
| Column Total | 76 | 45 | 141 | 162 | 424 |

| **Chi-Square** | **Value** | **DF** | **Significance** |
|---|---|---|---|
| Pearson | 30.39240 | 15 | 0.01058 |
| Pearson's R | 0.12084 | | |

**TABLE – 5.5**

**Family Type and Income (Annual)**

| Count<br>Exp. Val. | Income in Groups (Rs.) | | | | Row Total |
|---|---|---|---|---|---|
| | ≤ 25000 | 25001-50000 | 50001-1 lakh | Above 1 lakh | |
| Single | 6<br>8.3 | 45<br>35.3 | 56<br>58.5 | 22<br>27.0 | 129 |
| Joint | 8<br>13.6 | 52<br>57.8 | 102<br>95.5 | 49<br>44.2 | 211 |
| Nuclear | 13<br>5.1 | 18<br>21.9 | 32<br>36.2 | 17<br>16.8 | 80 |
| Column Total | 27 | 115 | 190 | 88 | 100.0 |

| <u>Chi-Square</u> | <u>Value</u> | <u>DF</u> | <u>Significance</u> |
|---|---|---|---|
| Pearson | 21.33320 | 6 | 0.00160 |
| Pearson's R | -0.03978 | | |

**TABLE – 5.6**

**Family Type and Occupation Status**

| Count<br>Exp. Val. | Occupation Status of the Family | | | | Row Total |
|---|---|---|---|---|---|
| | Ordinary | Industrial | Non-Industrial | Mixed | |
| Single | 39<br>23.1 | 31<br>13.7 | 36<br>42.9 | 23<br>49.3 | 129 |
| Joint | 24<br>38.4 | 6<br>22.7 | 72<br>71.2 | 112<br>81.8 | 214 |
| Nuclear | 13<br>14.5 | 8<br>8.6 | 33<br>26.9 | 27<br>30.9 | 81 |
| Column Total | 76 | 45 | 141 | 162 | 424 |

| <u>Chi-Square</u> | <u>Value</u> | <u>DF</u> | <u>Significance</u> |
|---|---|---|---|
| Pearson | 78.84710 | 6 | 0.00000 |
| Pearson's R | 0.23275 | | |

**TABLE – 5.7**

**Ideal Family Size and Income (Annual)**

| Persons Count Exp. Val. | Income in Groups (Rs.) | | | | Row Total |
|---|---|---|---|---|---|
| | ≤ 25000 | 25001-50000 | 50001-1 lakh | Above 1 lakh | |
| Nil | 11<br>13.8 | 61<br>58.9 | 109<br>97.3 | 34<br>45.0 | 215 |
| Three | 2<br>1.5 | 3<br>6.3 | 12<br>10.4 | 6<br>4.8 | 23 |
| Four | 8<br>8.6 | 34<br>36.4 | 52<br>60.2 | 39<br>27.9 | 133 |
| Five | 5<br>2.3 | 11<br>9.9 | 13<br>16.3 | 7<br>7.5 | 36 |
| Six | 1<br>0.8 | 6<br>3.6 | 4<br>5.9 | 2<br>2.7 | 13 |
| Column Total | 27 | 115 | 190 | 88 | 420 |

| Chi-Square | Value | DF | Significance |
|---|---|---|---|
| Pearson | 19.42662 | 12 | 0.07874 |
| Pearson's R | -0.00124 | | |

**TABLE – 5.8**

**Ideal Family Size and Occupation Status**

| Person Count Exp. Val. | Occupation Status of the Family | | | | Row Total |
|---|---|---|---|---|---|
| | Ordinary | Industrial | Non-Industrial | Mixed | |
| Nil | 29<br>39.1 | 3<br>23.1 | 63<br>72.5 | 123<br>83.3 | 218 |
| Three | 9<br>4.1 | 3<br>2.4 | 7<br>7.6 | 4<br>8.8 | 23 |
| Four | 34<br>24.0 | 33<br>14.2 | 46<br>44.6 | 21<br>51.2 | 134 |
| Five | 3<br>6.5 | 1<br>3.8 | 22<br>12.0 | 10<br>13.8 | 36 |
| Six | 1<br>2.3 | 5<br>1.4 | 3<br>4.3 | 4<br>5.0 | 13 |
| Column Total | 76 | 45 | 141 | 162 | 424 |

| **Chi-Square** | **Value** | **DF** | **Significance** |
|---|---|---|---|
| Pearson | 119.86661 | 12 | 0.00000 |
| Pearson's R | -0.30319 | | |

**TABLE – 5.9**

**Total Children and Education**

| Total Children Count Exp. Val. | Family Education Yrs. of Schooling (Highest) | | | | | Row Total |
|---|---|---|---|---|---|---|
| | Illiterate | Primary | High School | Higher Sec. | College | |
| Nil | 10<br>3.3 | 5<br>5.1 | 4<br>13.2 | 11<br>10.6 | 15<br>12.8 | 45 |
| One | 4<br>5.3 | 8<br>8.2 | 28<br>21.1 | 14<br>17.0 | 18<br>20.5 | 72 |
| Two | 7<br>12.1 | 16<br>18.7 | 42<br>48.3 | 51<br>38.9 | 49<br>47.1 | 165 |
| Three | 5<br>6.9 | 13<br>10.8 | 33<br>27.8 | 18<br>22.4 | 26<br>27.1 | 95 |
| Four | 4<br>1.8 | 1<br>2.7 | 9<br>7.0 | 5<br>5.7 | 5<br>6.8 | 24 |
| Five | 1<br>1.7 | 5<br>2.6 | 8<br>6.7 | 1<br>5.4 | 8<br>6.6 | 23 |
| Column Total | 31 | 48 | 124 | 100 | 121 | 424 |

| <u>**Chi-Square**</u> | <u>**Value**</u> | <u>**DF**</u> | <u>**Significance**</u> |
|---|---|---|---|
| Pearson | 45.66970 | 20 | 0.00089 |
| Pearson's R | 0.02294 | | |

**TABLE – 5.10**

**Total Children and Education Expense**

| Total Children Count Exp. Val. | Annual Expense of Education Per Child (Rs.) | | | | | Row Total |
|---|---|---|---|---|---|---|
| | Nil. | 1-500 | 501-1000 | 1001-2000 | 2001-3000 | |
| One | 38<br>19.8 | 2<br>15.0 | 9<br>14.6 | 8<br>12.0 | 4<br>6.1 | 72 |
| Two | 43<br>45.3 | 30<br>34.4 | 32<br>33.5 | 32<br>27.4 | 23<br>13.9 | 165 |
| Three | 12<br>26.1 | 26<br>19.8 | 27<br>19.3 | 20<br>15.8 | 3<br>8.0 | 95 |
| Four | 4<br>6.6 | 10<br>5.0 | 5<br>4.9 | 3<br>4.0 | 1<br>2.0 | 24 |
| Five | 7<br>6.3 | 11<br>4.8 | 4<br>4.7 | 0<br>3.8 | 1<br>1.9 | 23 |
| Column Total | 104 | 79 | 77 | 63 | 32 | 379 |

| Chi-Square | Value | DF | Significance |
|---|---|---|---|
| Pearson | 89.58514 | 20 | 0.00000 |
| Pearson's R | -0.05022 | | |

**TABLE – 5.11**

**Ideal Family Size and Education**

| Person Count Exp. Val. | Family Education Yrs. of Schooling (Highest) | | | | | Row Total |
|---|---|---|---|---|---|---|
| | Illiterate | Primary | High School | Higher Sec. | College | |
| Nil | 12<br>15.9 | 18<br>24.7 | 84<br>63.8 | 69<br>51.4 | 35<br>62.2 | 218 |
| Three | 24<br>1.7 | 28<br>2.6 | 4<br>6.7 | 5<br>5.4 | 10<br>6.6 | 23 |
| Four | 15<br>9.8 | 19<br>15.2 | 24<br>39.2 | 18<br>31.6 | 58<br>38.2 | 134 |
| Five | 0<br>2.6 | 6<br>4.1 | 11<br>10.5 | 6<br>8.5 | 13<br>10.3 | 36 |
| Six | 2<br>1.0 | 31<br>1.5 | 1<br>3.8 | 25<br>3.1 | 5<br>3.7 | 13 |
| Column Total | 31 | 48 | 124 | 100 | 121 | 424 |

| Chi-Square | Value | DF | Significance |
|---|---|---|---|
| Pearson | 66.59365 | 16 | 0.00000 |
| Pearson's R | 0.03813 | | |

**TABLE – 5.12**

**Total Children and Religion**

| Total Children Count Exp. Val. | Religion | | | Row Total |
|---|---|---|---|---|
| | Hindu | Muslim | Other | |
| Nil | 41<br>39.8 | 4<br>3.5 | 0<br>1.7 | 45 |
| One | 64<br>63.7 | 6<br>5.6 | 2<br>2.7 | 72 |
| Two | 152<br>145.9 | 6<br>12.8 | 7<br>6.2 | 165 |
| Three | 79<br>84.0 | 13<br>7.4 | 3<br>3.6 | 95 |
| Four | 21<br>21.2 | 1<br>1.9 | 2<br>0.9 | 24 |
| Five | 18<br>20.3 | 3<br>1.8 | 2<br>0.9 | 23 |
| Column Total | 375 | 33 | 16 | 424 |

| Chi-Square | Value | DF | Significance |
|---|---|---|---|
| Pearson | 14.95580 | 10 | 0.13368 |
| Pearson's R | 0.10278 | | |

## TABLE – 5.13

**Ideal Family Size and Religion**

| Person Count Exp. Val. | Religion | | | Row Total |
|---|---|---|---|---|
| | Hindu | Muslim. | Other | |
| Nil | 210<br>192.8 | 5<br>17.0 | 3<br>8.2 | 218 |
| Three | 19<br>20.3 | 2<br>1.8 | 2<br>0.9 | 23 |
| Four | 111<br>118.5 | 14<br>10.4 | 9<br>5.1 | 134 |
| Five | 26<br>31.8 | 9<br>2.8 | 1<br>1.4 | 36 |
| Six | 9<br>11.5 | 3<br>1.0 | 1<br>0.5 | 13 |
| Column Total | 375 | 33 | 16 | 424 |

| Chi-Square | Value | DF | Significance |
|---|---|---|---|
| Pearson | 39.51319 | 8 | 0.00000 |
| Pearson's R | 0.23882 | | |

**TABLE – 5.14**

**Total Children and Migration**

| Total Children<br>Count<br>Exp. Val. | Migration | | Row<br>Total |
|---|---|---|---|
| | Native | Migrant | |
| Nil | 35<br>32.8 | 10<br>12.2 | 45 |
| One | 50<br>52.5 | 22<br>19.5 | 72 |
| Two | 116<br>120.2 | 49<br>44.8 | 165 |
| Three | 74<br>69.2 | 21<br>25.8 | 22.4 |
| Four | 15<br>17.5 | 9<br>6.5 | 24 |
| Five | 19<br>16.8 | 4<br>6.2 | 23 |
| Column<br>Total | 309 | 115 | 424 |

| **Chi-Square** | **Value** | **DF** | **Significance** |
|---|---|---|---|
| Pearson | 5.14857 | 5 | 0.39802 |
| Pearson's R | -0.01963 | | |

**TABLE – 5.15**

**Ideal Family Size and Migration**

| Person Count<br>Exp. Val. | Migration<br>Native | <br>Migrant | Row<br>Total |
|---|---|---|---|
| Nil | 148<br>158.9 | 70<br>59.1 | 218 |
| Three | 18<br>16.8 | 5<br>6.2 | 23 |
| Four | 102<br>97.7 | 32<br>36.3 | 134 |
| Five | 29<br>26.2 | 7<br>9.8 | 36 |
| Six | 12<br>9.5 | 1<br>3.5 | 13 |
| Column Total | 309 | 115 | 424 |

| Chi-Square | Value | DF | Significance |
|---|---|---|---|
| Pearson | 7.34994 | 4 | 0.11851 |
| Pearson's R | -0.12346 | | |

**TABLE – 5.16**

**Family Type and Migration**

| Count<br>Exp. Val. | Migration<br>Native | <br>Migrant | Row<br>Total |
|---|---|---|---|
| Single | 108<br>94.0 | 21<br>35.0 | 129 |
| Joint | 150<br>156.0 | 64<br>58.0 | 214 |
| Nuclear | 51<br>59.0 | 30<br>22.0 | 81 |
| Column Total | 309 | 115 | 424 |

| Chi-Square | Value | DF | Significance |
|---|---|---|---|
| Pearson | 12.54089 | 2 | 0.00189 |
| Pearson's R | 0.16816 | | |

**TABLE – 5.17**

**Total Children and Ideal Family Size***

| Total Children Count Exp. Val. | Ideal Family Size (Persons) | | | | | Row Total |
|---|---|---|---|---|---|---|
| | 0 | 3 | 4 | 5 | 6 | |
| Nil | 24<br>23.1 | 6<br>2.4 | 13<br>14.2 | 1<br>3.8 | 1<br>1.4 | 45 |
| One | 34<br>37.0 | 12<br>3.9 | 24<br>22.8 | 2<br>6.1 | 0<br>2.2 | 72 |
| Two | 91<br>84.8 | 1<br>9.0 | 67<br>52.1 | 4<br>14.0 | 2<br>5.1 | 165 |
| Three | 46<br>48.8 | 2<br>5.2 | 18<br>30.0 | 27<br>8.1 | 2<br>2.9 | 95 |
| Four | 15<br>12.3 | 1<br>1.3 | 5<br>7.6 | 0<br>2.0 | 3<br>0.7 | 24 |
| Five | 8<br>11.8 | 1<br>1.2 | 7<br>7.3 | 2<br>2.0 | 5<br>0.7 | 23 |
| Column Total | 218 | 23 | 134 | 36 | 13 | 424 |

* Parents + Children

| Chi-Square | Value | DF | Significance |
|---|---|---|---|
| Pearson | 139.94464 | 20 | 0.00000 |
| Pearson's R | 0.10160 | | |

**TABLE – 5.18**

**Total Children and Family Type**

| Total Children<br>Count<br>Exp. Val. | Family Type<br>Single | <br>Joint | <br>Nuclear | Row<br>Total |
|---|---|---|---|---|
| Nil | 20<br>13.7 | 19<br>22.7 | 6<br>8.6 | 45 |
| One | 30<br>21.9 | 30<br>36.3 | 12<br>13.8 | 72 |
| Two | 51<br>50.2 | 87<br>83.3 | 27<br>31.5 | 165 |
| Three | 21<br>28.9 | 48<br>47.9 | 26<br>18.1 | 95 |
| Four | 4<br>7.3 | 16<br>12.1 | 4<br>4.6 | 24 |
| Five | 3<br>7.0 | 14<br>11.6 | 6<br>4.4 | 23 |
| Column<br>Total | 129 | 214 | 81 | 424 |

| **Chi-Square** | **Value** | **DF** | **Significance** |
|---|---|---|---|
| Pearson | 21.18292 | 10 | 0.01985 |
| Pearson's R | 0.18089 | | |

**TABLE – 5.19**

**Ideal Family Size and Family Type**

| Person Count Exp. Val. | Family Type | | | Row Total |
|---|---|---|---|---|
| | Single | Joint | Nuclear | |
| Nil | 39<br>66.3 | 160<br>110.0 | 19<br>41.6 | 218 |
| Three | 13<br>7.0 | 5<br>11.6 | 5<br>4.4 | 23 |
| Four | 66<br>40.8 | 30<br>67.6 | 38<br>25.6 | 134 |
| Five | 8<br>11.0 | 12<br>18.2 | 16<br>6.9 | 36 |
| Six | 3<br>4.0 | 7<br>6.6 | 3<br>2.5 | 13 |
| Column Total | 129 | 214 | 81 | 424 |

| **Chi-Square** | **Value** | **DF** | **Significance** |
|---|---|---|---|
| Pearson | 113.18372 | 8 | 0.00000 |
| Pearson's R | 0.00268 | | |

**TABLE – 5.20**

**Housing Conditions and Income (Annual)**

| Count Exp. Val. | Family Income in Groups (Rs.) | | | | Row Total |
|---|---|---|---|---|---|
| | ≤ 25000 | 25001-50000 | 50001-1 lakh | 1-2 lakh | |
| Own | 23<br>23.7 | 96<br>100.8 | 167<br>166.5 | 82<br>77.1 | 368 |
| Rented | 4<br>3.3 | 19<br>14.2 | 23<br>23.5 | 6<br>10.9 | 52 |
| Column Total | 27 | 115 | 190 | 88 | 420 |

| **Chi-Square** | **Value** | **DF** | **Significance** |
|---|---|---|---|
| Pearson | 4.48862 | 3 | 0.21331 |
| Pearson's R | -0.08424 | | |

# CHAPTER – VI

# SUMMARY AND POLICY IMPLICATIONS

This concluding chapter is an attempt to summarize the discussions of the previous chapters. The chapter also attempts to discuss broad implications and limitations of the study and indicates the future scope for further study in the population related area.

First chapter deals with the importance and relevance of the study and the existing status of the subject under consideration. The objectives and the hypotheses of the study are discussed in detail in this introductory chapter.

A detailed discussion of various population theories is undertaken in the second chapter. The enumerated population theories are Pre-Malthusian theories, Malthusian theory, Biological theories, Socio-cultural theories and Economic theories. It has also been attempted to seek the relevance of the population theories discussed here with the subject of this thesis. Some of the hypotheses have been derived from the population theories that are to be tested later on.

Chapter third provides an overview of socio-economic characteristics and demographic profile of India, Gujarat and Surat. A conceptual framework was initially prepared before undertaking the discussion on this chapter. Some of the important socio-economic variables like religion, education, income, IMR, CMR, expenditure on children's education, health, family planning, duration and causes of migration etc. have been elaborately discussed in this chapter as these are the variables affecting population growth. Secondary data available from different sources have been used for this purpose.

Methodology of data collection and data analysis and the description of the sample households are given in the fourth chapter. The social, economical and demographic characteristics of the study area – Surat – are discussed in this chapter. The results based on the primary data have been analysed to derive the findings of the study. Discussion on the statistical techniques employed for this analysis is also included in this chapter.

Empirical analysis of micro determinants of population growth is presented in the fifth chapter. The chapter deals with the empirical analysis carried out to test the hypotheses. It has been attempted to examine the association between variables using chi-square analysis and cross table examinations. Some of the results of this analysis have been found to agree with the results of the previous studies conducted by researchers in the similar areas. Some of the results of the present analysis differ from the results of the previous studies. These results might prove to be quite useful to future researchers who would like to pursue study in the similar field.

Time and again, it has been seen that in the process of urbanization demographic changes take place along with socio-economic development. The changes in population bring about changes in quality and quantity of population. Migration also affects a great deal on the changing pattern of population growth in urban areas. Birth, death and migration – these three factors are important in the study of population growth and development. It has been observed that in the initial phase of urbanization large-scale migration takes place drastically increasing the pressure of population of the area affected. After this initial phase, the increase in population takes place in its natural course but the rate of population growth reduces. In the third and final phase, the cycle of socio-economic development of an urban area completes a full circle. The people who migrate to the cities from various socio-eco-cultural backgrounds gradually adapt themselves to the new place and in a long run; they become inseparable part of the city. Hence, these migrants who came to Surat before 25 years have not been considered as migrants. They are included in the study as urban natives.

The physical area of the present study is the industrial city of Surat situated on the banks of the river Tapi in South Gujarat region of India. In 1991, the population of Surat was 1498817. In 2001, it was 2433765. In the present study, 2080 individual out of the total population living in 424 households have been covered. There are 979 women against 1101 men. Out of these sample households, 88.4 per cent are Hindus and 7.8 per cent are Muslims. The proportion of migrant households is 27.1 per cent.

There are 889 females per thousand males in Surat. The average marriageable age is 19.52 for women and 23.54 for men. The average marriageable age of both men and women is 21.51. This means the average marriageable age is higher in population of Surat compared to legal marriageable age. And still marriages below legal marriageable age do take place in Surat. The proportion of women getting married before the legal age is 24.85 per cent while in men it is 17.80 per cent. It has been observed from the results of this study that at least one fourth of the total numbers of women are still married off before 18 years. To prevent the marriages at younger age the following measures can be suggested: (i) It should be made compulsory to register marriages. (ii) Steps should be taken to increase the proportion of education in females. (iii) Voluntary pressure groups should be formed to check child and under age marriage.

The total period of marriage, the spousal age difference and desired family size – these three are the major factors affecting fertility. The average period of marriage in the sample population has been found to be 13.8 years, while spousal age difference is 4.16 and desired family size is 4.27 persons. The average rate of children ever born in Surat is 2.22 and the survival rate of children is 2.20. The figures indicate that 99.10 per cent of children survive. The findings indicate rapid decrease in CMR. Another important indicator of the findings is that the average number of female children is lower than male children, which might be a problem of serious concern.

Along with the average period of marriage and average spousal age difference the average birth rate in Surat is 2.22, which indicates that the average gap between two births is five to six years. The average number of children in migrants is 2.16, while it was 2.24 before they migrated to Surat. This is a clear indicator that even in migrant population fertility rate is not higher than the fertility rate in native urban population. This shows that the present growth of population is not due to migration but it is natural. The gap between birth rate and death rate in Surat is considerably wider because death rate is just 4.33 against 16.35 birth rate.

More than 90 per cent of households are found to be aware of family planning programme implemented by the Government to control population growth in the city. Though all these 92.2 households believe in family planning, only 76.7 per cent households have accepted family planning.

The contribution of family doctors and Primary Health Centres (41.54 per cent and 36.92 per cent respectively) in imparting knowledge of family planning and bringing about awareness of family planning among the people is quite noteworthy. The permanent family planning has been adopted by 61.23 per cent couples. In temporary methods of family planning, males generally prefer condoms (45.24 per cent) while females opt for oral pills (22.22 per cent). Of course, men do not readily adopt permanent family planning. Only 4.52 per cent (Table - 6.1) men have opted for vasectomy while 95.48 per cent women have been operated upon for permanent sterilization. People have preferred private clinics (62.61 per cent) for this purpose. Only 35.68 per cent have availed of the facilities provided by Public Health Centres and a mere 2.1 per cent took the help from medical camps.

In the result of the classification of eligible married women below the age of 24 years who (Table - 6.1) accepted family planning, 60.52 per cent are included. If the eligible couples who fall in this category of age actually get married at the legal age of marriage, 5.90 per cent decrease can be brought about in eligible couples. If girls prefer to acquire education up to post graduation, their average age at marriage will go higher. This will help to limit the total period of fertility in women. If a temporary method of family planning is adopted by a still larger number of women, number of children in a family will still decrease. Minimum use of temporary methods of family planning is found in low-income group of people. They generally prefer operations for family planning. Even in this class of people, it is women who go for such operations. If they can be made aware of the temporary methods and their proper uses, their married life can be healthier and they can plan their family.

A family's attitude towards health care is reflected in the manner children are looked after and brought up by parents. The study indicates that 90.3 per cent households possess the knowledge of immunization. The proportion of families who have immunized their children is 86.4 per cent but only 55.08 per cent, i.e. a little more than 50 per cent, have completed the full immunization programme prescribed by WHO for the well being of children.

People prefer to get their children immunized from private clinics. Average annual expenditure on health care is merely Rs.1467. Low income families generally seek medical help from clinics run by charitable trusts or Government hospitals. If more families go for immunization of their children, it will positively affect family planning. To make immunization successful, door-to-door propaganda and some kind of motivation are still needed. Parents should be made aware of the importance of Record Card of their children's immunization programme.

It has been found that in our society parents still prefer male child. This may be one of the reasons why the proportion of male children is quite high in the families having only one child. Parents still prefer to provide better educational facilities to their male children (27.8 per cent). Parents prefer to give higher education to their sons, hence 37 per cent parents wish to make their sons graduate while 30 per cent parents also wish to provide higher education to their daughters. As far as post graduation level education is concerned, 38.7 per cent parents wish their sons to go for post graduation, while only 26.5 per cent parents want their daughters to achieve post graduation. It seems that lack of higher education in the heads of households is responsible for this partial attitude towards sons. If the head of family is educated, change in this type of attitude is possible. Higher education in female children will also bring about another desirable change in society.

Automatically their marriageable age will go high and this will shorten the period of fertility in women.

The study of housing condition in Surat shows that 2.55 persons in Surat live in single room. More than 75 per cent households (86.8 per cent) possess their own houses. There are 75.5 per cent pucca houses while 24.6 per cent kuchcha houses. Electricity is available to almost all households (96.5 per cent) but many of the households do not possess separate kitchen and sanitation (64.8 pre cent and 78.3 per cent respectively). It is a pressing need that 100 per cent of households should be provided with proper sanitation for the sake of public health and social welfare. The SMC has tried to mitigate the problem by providing Sulabh sanitary complexes. Though 60.8 per cent households easily get drinking water, 64.8 per cent of the total households have to rely upon public taps for water. It has been derived that education or religion does not affect the housing condition of the households but income, family type and status of family do affect the housing condition.

To show the interrelationship between two variables cross tables are used in the analysis in chapter - V. With the help of chi square analysis, significant value is found of each variable. If significant value is found to the less than one per cent, it indicates that two variables are highly inter-related. If significant value is below 5 per cent, it indicates 95 per cent co-relation between the variables. The tables prepared are based on the hypotheses indicated in chapter - I and then it has been tried to examine whether or not hypotheses are correct and acceptable. Total number of children in a household and other factors are analysed in the tables separately.

The results of the tables indicate some of the interesting derivations. In the households where total number of children is more, number of girl children is also more. From the above example, it can be discerned that more female children are added to the family in expectation of a male child. (i) There are 42.97 per cent households having only male children. (ii) Families having only one male child are 15.65 per cent. (iii) There are two or more than two female children in 33.50 per cent households.

If it is possible to wipe off the importance of male child from the minds of people it will be possible to control the number of children in a family. Education to women and equal opportunities to both male and female children can bring about these social changes.

Most of the individuals have opted for small family size. In the households where total number of children is less have opted for small family. Even those households having only daughters have also opined that the size of family should be small. This means that the households having daughters might have contained their family size if at least one son were born to them.

More than 50 per cent families (68.2 per cent) have only one earning member. In most households, men are earning members of the family. The average dependency ratio is 29.52 per cent, out or which 25.58 per cent are senior citizens above 60 years of age. The average annual income in most families is Rs.60,000. Minimum annual income is Rs.5000. The relationship between income, occupational status and fertility are shown in Chapter - V. The results indicate that there is no correlation between total number of children and income of household. There are many other factors affecting the number of children in households living in an urban area like Surat. It has been noted that occupational status of a household affects the total number of children in a family. The number of children is more in mixed and non-industrial households. Households living in joint family system possess more income. Most families having mixed occupational status live in joint families. Income is not an important factor in deciding the number of children in a family, but it is the occupational status of the households and individual opinion regarding ideal family size responsible in deciding the number of children. Individuals living in mixed families have opted for large number of children in their families.

Economic activity and not actual income affect fertility of people living in an urban area. People expect to get some kind of job in a city. Rate of education and category of education also affects fertility. It has been examined that the number of children is less in the household having higher education. Educated people do not prefer to live in joint family system. The number of children is less in the households where parents have to spend more on their children's education. The households having maximum education upto high school level believe that five members is the ideal family size.

From the above stated analysis, it can be derived that the level and proportion of higher education should go high to limit the number of children in a household. Firstly, the level of education of head of the household should be high. An infrastructure should be created where parents have to spend less money after their children's education. If parents do not have to spend large amount and their children's education, automatically the level of education will go high and high education will help control the number of children.

The impact of religion on fertility in the urban area is almost negligible. The results of this study also indicate that there is no association between religion and number of children. There is no striking difference in the number of children either in Hindus or Muslims or in the families with any other faith. Most religions neither dictate their followers to live in separate families nor do they recommend checking the family size. However, the findings of this study show that all people in the urban area wish to educate their children irrespective of their religious beliefs. Eventually they prefer to marry only after completion of their studies. Even those individuals who are not fortunate enough to acquire education are engaged is economic activities to support their parents, hence they also prefer marriage after gaining economic stability. Naturally, they do not become parents at early age.

The opinion regarding the ideal size of family among the migrants is not much different from that of the urban natives. The demographic constitution of Surat city is of mixed type. It is not very easy now to separate the natives from the migrants. Those migrants who migrated to Surat years ago are now through and through urban natives in all respects. The pattern of life of the migrants indicates that in the initial years of their migration, they prefer joint family system but afterwards they start living as single families.

The relationship between the total numbers of children in a household, the individuals opinions regarding ideal family size and the type of families have been discussed in chapter – V in greater details. It has been observed that the total number of children is more in the households living in joint families compared to all other family types. The parents in the households having large number of children have opined for large number of children in the family, while parent in the households having small number of children opted for small family size.

Chapter - IV mainly deals with the explanation of results derived from the primary data while chapter five shows the number of children in a family (fertility) in relation with various other factors. The fifth chapter shows the impact of different variables on fertility and derives results with the help of chi square analysis method. The general conclusions arrived at in both these chapter are as follows:

1. The total of females is less than males.
2. The proportion of marriage at young age is 21.79 per cent.
3. The proportion of marriage at young age is higher in females than in males.
4. The average years of marriage is 13.18 years.
5. Most respondents believe that ideal family size should be 4.27 persons.
6. The average spousal age difference is 4.16 years.
7. The average of ever born children per household is 2.22.
8. Survival rate in the children ever born is 2.20.
9. Migrants give birth to less number of children after their migration.
10. The total of 76.2 per cent households in Surat have adopted family planning.
11. More females adopt permanent family planning than males.
12. The role of family doctor is important in imparting the knowledge of family planning.
13. Most operations for family planning are done in private clinics.
14. Parents still want to provide better education to their sons and not to their daughters.
15. There are no major problems of drinking water, electricity and clean air but proper housing is a considerable problem in Surat.
16. In 55.08 per cent of households, children are fully immunized.

17. Birth rate is 16.75 per cent while death rate is 4.33 per cent.
18. In the families having large number of children, the number of girl children is high.
19. There is only one earning members in 68.2 per cent households.
20. The dependency ratio in Surat is 29.52 per cent in which majority are children.
21. There is no co-relationship between income and number of children in a household.
22. Household's occupational status plays vital role in deciding the number of children.
23. High education – not total education in a family checks the number of children.
24. High expenditure on education per child limits the total number of children in a household.
25. The impact of religion on the number of children is negligible.
26. Religion preaches joint family system.
27. The average number of children per household is almost equal both in migrant households and urban native households.
28. Migrant families posses mixed occupational status.
29. Migrants initially prefer joint family system.
30. Migrant couples give birth to less number of children after migration.
31. The number of children is more in joint families.

32. The opinion of respondents regarding the ideal family size is almost similar.

**Limitations**

This study is based on micro level study using primary data. It will be useful to note some of the limitations this researcher has come across during the analysis of the collected data from the households. The limitations are as follow:

(i) As many as 85 per cent of the households could be contacted from the total households selected for this study. Fifteen per cent of the households could not be approached due to some unavoidable reasons. Because of this limitation, certain areas have not been included in the data.

(ii) The households were not selected on the basis of caste/creed, yet proportion of Hindu/ Muslim population has been observed. Still Parsis are completely left out from the study not deliberately, but because of random sampling. Their population is gradually declining. It will require a separate study to look into the problems of declining population of Parsis.

(iii) It has been attempted to examine the effects of socio-economic factors affecting population growth in the present study but the influence of caste has not been considered.

(iv) It has been difficult to collect data regarding child as an asset because families were unwilling to provide such information.

(v) It has been noticed that people living in the urban area already know what is the legal marriageable age for male and female but parents were not willing to provide information whether marriages of their off springs took place at an younger age. Due to the respondents' unwillingness to provide the correct information, it has been difficult to find the average of child marriages between the age of thirteen and eighteen years. This limitation has been detected while cross-examining the collected data of mothers' age at the birth of their first child.

(vi) It was difficult to obtain quantitative information of the household expenditure pattern because people could not provide the exact information about the consumption of the average quantity of food grains, vegetable, edible oils etc. However, it was possible to obtain information about the total average expenditure.

(vii) It has been difficult to obtain reliable family information about the people who have migrated to Surat from the nearby villages for the following reasons; (a) They were unwilling to provide information about the size, status and income of the family. (b) The service class people living in Surat enjoy high standard of living yet they were unwilling to show their income obtained from agriculture. (c) Though such families live in Surat, they can be better classed as floating population.

(viii) It was difficult to obtain information about the use of the temporary methods of contraception because of two reasons: (a) Most of those residing in slums do not have any knowledge of the temporary contraceptive methods. (b) The middle class and upper class people who use these devices were not willing to provide such information.

(ix) Single-family type and nuclear family type are both classed under single category though there is a minor difference between the two. Those couples who start living separately from their parental house soon after marriage and form their separate family are called nuclear families.

(x) All respondents were not willing to speak frankly about their concept regarding the ideal family type/ size.

(xi) In the analysis of the effects of family type on the number of children, only two categories of family type are given consideration: (1) Joint family type and (2) others inclusive of single/ nuclear family type.

**Scope for Future Study**

The present study is one step further in the field of population study. The area of research in population related studies is very vast. Several studies on population related problems have been undertaken by scholars. They have enriched and expanded the field of research. The investigator of the present study believes that this study might become quite useful to the future scholars. Some of the scopes of this type of population studies are as follows:

(i) This type of researches is important for comparative studies. Socio-economic and demographic features of the ever expanding and progressing city like Surat do not remain constant for a long time. The findings of this research might become useful to future studies on demographic characteristics of Surat city.

(ii) A comparative study of any other city of Gujarat can be taken up with the help of the data and results of this study.

(iii) A comparative study of socio-economically prosperous cities of different states can be compared with the present study.

## TABLE – 6.1 (A)

**Different Planning Methods Used by Eligible Couples**

| Bride Age | Eligible Couple | Male Operation | Female Operation | Copper 'T' | Condom used | Oral Pills | Other Methods | Total |
|---|---|---|---|---|---|---|---|---|
| 15-19 | 25 | -- | -- | 3 | 5 | 5 | 1 | 14 |
| 20-24 | 89 | -- | 23 | 7 | 15 | 7 | 3 | 55 |
| 25-29 | 98 | 2 | 48 | 5 | 16 | 10 | 4 | 85 |
| 30-34 | 100 | 3 | 49 | 5 | 9 | 4 | 4 | 74 |
| 35-39 | 72 | 3 | 46 | 3 | 7 | 1 | 2 | 62 |
| 40-49 | 40 | 1 | 24 | 2 | 5 | 1 | 2 | 35 |
| Total | 424 | 9 | 190 | 25 | 57 | 28 | 16 | 325 |

## TABLE – 6.1 (B)

| Wife's Age | Eligible Couple | List F.P. Methods used by couples | Not a single method used |
|---|---|---|---|
| 15-19 | 25 | 14 | 11 |
| 20-24 | 89 | 55 | 34 |
| 25-29 | 98 | 85 | 13 |
| 30-34 | 100 | 74 | 26 |
| 35-39 | 72 | 62 | 10 |
| 40-49 | 40 | 35 | 05 |
| Total | 424 | 325 | 99 |

CPSIA information can be obtained
at www.ICGtesting.com
Printed in the USA
LVHW021320031222
734485LV00013B/940

9 781805 452256